1

The absence of a bibliography is due to the fact that the vast majority of information contained in this book has been gathered freely on route. Sources include tour guides, tourist information centers and knowledgeable locals. I cannot guarantee that all the facts are correct.

Although the people in the book are real, I must confess to having somewhat embellished their characters. My apologies if any offence is caused.

# CHICAGO-KEY LARGO

## American Road trip

### Trevor Lane

For my lovely family,

"Adhere to your purpose and you will soon feel as well as you ever did. On the contrary, if you falter, and give up, you will lose the power of keeping any resolution, and will regret it all your life."

*Abraham Lincoln.*

# _Preface_

One of the mildly frustrating things about being a human being is that I never get to find out if other people's brains function in the same way as mine.

I muddle through life with what feels like a head full of light mist transforming to fog on a bad day. However every now and then, but nowhere near often enough, the fog dissipates and I get to experience a 'moment of clarity'. They arrive usually after a period of rest in which the brain has had time to filter out the white noise of everyday life.

This book was written during several brief moments of clarity and I thank my wife for allowing me the luxury of being buffered from the world during this period. Oh yes, and for letting me blow some of our hard earned cash on a trip with the lads xxx.

# One

When I first heard about the concept of the bucket list, I have to admit that my immediate reaction was one of disdain. Was this just another forced internet craze akin to drowning in iced water or photographing one's anatomy in a sock?

Upon reflection, for my age group it actually made a lot of sense. Anything that pushes us away from the sometimes unavoidably mundane drudgery commonly labeled as every-day-life, is surely a positive thing. If I am to be forced into anything in the years that rest, let it be something that I have always wanted to do. As a young man I felt that I was time rich, a whole lifetime ahead of me. Like everybody else I was happy to sell my time to the highest bidder, in return for the things that one expects from life; a car, a home, a television. As the years advance, time becomes far more valuable than money and the only way to ensure that dreams become reality is to make a plan. A plan long enough to be viable but not so long as to run the very real risk of running out of time.

At the age of fifty my building work had dried up and my personal projects were all but finished. Something was telling me that this was my opportunity to pursue a different career path.

# *Two*

Travel writer at 51.......I can almost sense the mass accumulation of the electrical impulses responsible for the thought 'no spring chicken' form and dissipate in your collective brains. But the sad truth is that up until this point in my life I don't really think I've had that much to say. I was hesitating to insert the word 'interesting' in that sentence, but it's probably fairer if I let you be the judge of that.

Writing was never really a plan but more a continuation of a series of disjointed careers which includes failed rock star, carpenter, teacher, tour rep', waiter, barman and descends into the category of 'gains little respect or financial remuneration whilst managing to suck out all life and hope'.

If one isn't careful there is a tendency for life to stagnate after 50. Physically the best years have packed up and gone, leaving an active brain full of accumulated knowledge inside a vessel which is, quite frankly, not up to the job of fulfilling many bucket list wishes. So compromises have to be made. It is getting less likely that I will ever run marathons, scale the ten highest peaks, swim across the English Channel or other formidable bodies of water, sail the Mediterranean sea with a naked crew of aspiring models......I will stop there as I can imagine my daughters shouting in unison 'old perve' across the room, a phrase which I feel hits a little below the belt (pun intended). I would take this opportunity to say on behalf of all maturing men that just because we are knocking on a bit it doesn't necessarily mean that our taste in women changes. Can we not look at the young ladies and appreciate the same things we have always appreciated without being cold-shouldered by our wives and slandered by our daughters?? I think we know the answer to that one.

But I digress, there are many experiences still available on the list for someone of my age, some even daring, adventurous and challenging, well for me at least. Take for example the pilgrimage to Saint-Jacques-de-Compostelle. Starting in France, crossing the Pyrenees and heading west to pay homage to the mythical remains of Saint Jacques in the medieval town of Santiago de Compostelle. I've been thinking about this one for quite a while now but somehow I can't get past the thought of blisters on blisters. How about a spell in Peru following the legendary trail of the Incas, to feast one's eyes on the ancient city of Machu Picchu. I like the sound of this one and my wife does too which is always a good sign. Then there's Rio de Janeiro, the Amazon jungle, the Great Wall of China, Mount Kilimanjaro, the Burj Khalifa....the list goes on.

My list has been shortened due to my good fortune and, at the expense of any sort of career, I have managed to see quite a bit of the world already. However, where as it would be quite easy to rest on one's laurels, I am not willing to gamble with the possibility that I may have regrets on my death bed. I can see no other way to insure that I have done all within my power to avoid disappointment than to write a list, and funnily enough I start to feel more positive about life instantaneously.

# *Three*

I wonder if Alexander Graham Bell, or anyone else involved in piecing together the puzzle that resulted in the creation of telecommunications, had any idea of just how many life changing messages would be delivered in that fashion. In any case our adventure was spawned in just such a manner, a little after my 49th birthday.

Let me introduce you to my brother. He's 18 months older than me, has a good job in the city and he's doing very nicely thank you very much. That's not to say he doesn't deserve it, he has followed a chosen career path, he has worked very hard and now after many years he is reaping the benefits.

As he had never had much time for leisure travel he decided to mark his 50th year with, amongst other things, a trip to Australia. A year later and with his wife just back from a Himalayan trek with the ladies, he was looking to even up the score. So with my half century quickly approaching he took it upon himself (as older siblings invariably do) to ensuring that the event didn't pass by unmarked. After a boozy night out with his chum Neil, the not totally original idea of a road trip in the USA came up and I received that fateful call shortly after their headaches had worn off.

My reaction at first was one of rather forced enthusiasm due to a number of reasons. From an ethical point of view I have been known to feel guilty about my carbon foot print when making unnecessary journeys (that is until some smart arse pipes up with the cows and methane story which kind of poo poos this – pun intended); I'm not particularly captivated by cars and being in them; I have in my youth had the good fortune of seeing a fair number of states already, using a combination of Amtrak, Greyhound buses and sticking my thumb out by the side of the road. My final protestation was that there are other places I would rather go. When I gave this a little more thought it occurred to me that although there are many places on my always-wanted-to-go-and-see list there aren't many places on my regret-not-having-seen-as-I-take-my-last-breath       list. Elvis's mansion *Graceland* fell into the second category. Don't ask me why - it's not a rational thing and I am aware that it's just the house of a pop star. If someone were to propose a visit to the not so humble abode of, let's say, Britney Spears, my interest might stretch to mild curiosity but nowhere near enough to justify the several thousand mile jolly jaunt.

I don't really remember ever being a particular fan of Elvis. I guess the difference for me is that his life was the ultimate rock star story; rags to riches followed by tragic death. Our lives were intertwined from my earliest memories, seeing him in films dancing on a Hawaiian beach surrounded by a bevy of beauties or driving a convertible car through Hollywood America serenading a glamorous co-star.

I remember in the period just after his death, watching his 1968 comeback concert. He had been in Hollywood making films for so long that the thought of a live concert scared the life out of him. When he took to the stage in full leathers he seemed to me like the epitome of cool. Even for non-believers it was hard to deny the guy had enough talent and charisma to fill any stage or screen. When I got old enough to get served in pubs there would always be an Elvis fan present, usually the one with the sideburns, telling mythical stories about the life of the 'king'. His tragic death seemed to make him even more present with the re-release of all his old hits and newspapers full of stories telling tales of excess and eccentricity. With the advent of punk my musical tastes followed a different path but the legend of Mr. Presley continued to be told in songs such as 'Graceland', 'Walking in Memphis' and

'Black Velvet', poignant reminders that one day I would have to go and pay my respects.

However this wouldn't be the first time I've tried to get there. Twenty years ago I worked the summer as a waiter in Minnesota. At the end of the season I caught a ride with a friend as far as Iowa where I planned to make my way to Memphis, specifically to see 'Graceland'. During a routine base-touching phone call I learnt that my Grandmother was on her death bed, so for once I did the right thing - got the bus to Chicago and flew home to say goodbye.

In subsequent visits I have never got close enough to the state of Tennessee to make the hop to Memphis viable. I suggested this to my brother and the idea of a music based road trip was born; Chicago and Memphis blues, Nashville country followed by New Orleans jazz. Neil added Florida to the list as a place he loved to visit and we had our route.

Next we needed another team member on board as due to work commitments, Neil could only make the second half of the trip. My brother and I get on very well but I was slightly concerned that our relationship might be a little intense if we travelled alone for ten days. I put it down to the length of our fuses. My brother has a long fuse and mine is fairly short. My self-esteem is crying out for me to qualify this statement by saying there is no anatomical reference what so ever here (doth thou protest too much??). What I'm trying to say is that he tends to bottle things up for days and then  erupts like Mount Vesuvius, where as I am much more immediate in getting things off of my chest. By the way whilst we're on the subject of fuses an old lady in our choral society told me what I thought to be a rather good joke last week. She asked me "what is the similarity between a man and a snow fall?" I said I didn't know, looking at her blankly. Her response was "you never know how many inches you're going to get or how long it will last!"

We needed a diplomat to water our two man team down and I knew just the guy; my old friend Alex. As a fellow guitarist, collector of guitars, a lover of music and cars, a diplomat and an all round good bloke, he would make an invaluable contribution to the enjoyment of our trip.  He is also self employed and could give himself the three weeks (all be it unpaid) off of work. He was enthusiastic from the start, expressing an interest to visit the Gibson guitar factory en route adding to the musical theme.

There was one remaining hurdle to overcome, which to me was the most relevant and that was the subject of finance. I am blessed with a fairly large family and even though my wife earns enough to pay the bills my work prospects in rural France (where we reside) are at best sporadic. Whilst I keep busy with school runs and house maintenance and do jobs for people when I am asked, my financial contribution remains small. How could I justify spending what would amount to the following years family holiday budget on myself? The answer to that one was "I couldn't" and so for me the road trip would have to wait until such times as I could afford it, if ever.

Several months later I opened a birthday card from my brother to find a British Airways executive class ticket flying into Chicago and out of Miami for the following September. I couldn't believe it! All I can say is that I am blessed three fold: I have a brother, he has a good job and he has a big heart. The trip was on!

# *Four*

The obvious concept for the trip being music, I allowed myself to fantasize during the months prior to our departure. In Chicago I envisaged dimly lit bars filled with men in tilted fedora hats smoking Cuban cigars. The women would be elegant but sexy in tight fitting dresses, sucking on long cigarette holders and swaying to a phenomenal blues band. I imagined Nashville to be full of men wearing stepson hats, jeans covered by leather chaps and oversized shiny belt buckles, standing with their thumbs tucked into their belts. The women would be pretty, tanned southern girls in short dresses and cowboy boots, line dancing to next year's Garth Brooks. In Memphis I fantasized about small, sweaty honky-tonk bars serving Tennessee whisky by the bottle, with a seasoned rockabilly group giving the performance of their lives on a small stage in the corner. Needless to say my expectations were high.

Due to our time restraints we needed a structured trip, but at the same time decided that it would be nice to have enough freedom to add a little spontaneity along the way. We pre-booked hotels in Chicago, Memphis and New Orleans, leaving the rest to fate, an idea that in hindsight caused some unnecessary stress along the way due to the high demand for budget accommodation in some of the more popular towns. We also booked our trip to 'Sun Studios' and 'Graceland' as we were meeting some of my brother's friends there on a specific day. Apart from that, we had on our list of things to see, the town of Springfield; the 'Country Music Hall of Fame' and 'RCA Studios'; the 'Gibson' guitar factory; the 'Civil Rights Museum', a boat trip along the Mississippi river and an airboat ride in the Everglades. An added bonus for me was having our own transport. In previous trips by bus and train I never really got to see the rural, small town America celebrated in country music. I was curious to see if people really did dress like cowboys and drive beaten up 'Chevy' pickups.

My brother also had a personnel agenda. Living in middle class London surrounded by lycra clad fitness fanatics all making New Year's resolutions to give up everything but sweat and pain, he decided to make his own resolution to drink 365 different beers during the year. As supplies were already dwindling in his local area, he needed a new market to tap into. The USA, although not known in Europe for its artisanal beers, could add to his tally considerably.

# *Five*

The day of our departure arrived and we converged at my brother's house, being within a short taxi ride of Heathrow. On seeing the size of Alex's suit case, my first thought was that our trip was doomed from the start as it was unlikely that the plane would ever get off of the ground. He sheepishly explained that it was a 'going away' present from his wife and that even though he agreed it was little oversized, after such a loving gesture how could he not bring it? After sizing up the approximate volume of such a case and the quantity of worldly possessions one could fit within, I was inclined to wonder if she wanted him to come back...

The trip started well as even before we left Heathrow my brother managed to smuggle us in to the B.A. executive lounge. Before us a vast selection of breakfasts, reading material and alcohol to be enjoyed on comfortable sofas and sumptuous arm chairs - an experience of unimaginable luxury for your average    economy class ticket holder.

Entering the plane through the business class section it appeared that the main difference between them and us was the fact that their seats seemed to lie completely flat. The first class passengers disappeared upstairs into what I imagine resembles a scene from *Fantasy Island*. Sitting, sipping champagne (try and say that three times fast), feet dangling in a babbling brook, surrounded by lush tropical greenery with staff attending to their every whim. I will probably never find out, but as we were shown to our executive class seats, the advantages over my usual economy passage were overwhelming. The obvious difference being that we got more of everything; space, drinks, attention… with the glaring exception of the air hostess's posterior, which was mercifully smaller than the economy class version.

After a flurry of activity we found ourselves cruising nearly seven miles above the surface of the earth. Did I mention I hate flying? When I was young it didn't bother me in the slightest but now, with a wife and kids and responsibilities, the thought of plummeting into the sea scares the living crap out of me. Let's face it, they go through all the safety stuff and show us the life jackets, but I ask you, do you ever recall anybody that has experienced plummeting into the sea from thirty six thousand feet, appearing on daytime television to tell their story? Did anyone ever have the TV presenter in fits of laughter as they recounted a humorous anecdote about tripping down the inflatable slide into the welcoming life raft? I think we all know the answer to that one.

Nothing particularly interesting happened during the flight, barring me managing to dip one end of my useless fashion accessory of a 'hoody' cord, into my chicken chasseur sauce. The opposite cord suffered a similar fate during a visit to the joyless excuse for a plane toilet (which I'm sure by-the-way is shrinking, in a callous attempt to stop people joining that famous clique of altitude lovers.)
Anyway, whilst in the process of practicing the often questioned masculine art of multi-tasking; i.e. urinating with one hand whilst using the other to tear off a square or two of loo roll to blow my nose, I inadvertently caught a cord in the tissue on route to my hooter and gave a hearty blow. The result was not pretty but at least they matched now.

Being day time it was impossible to sleep during the flight so I contented myself with *Mad Max* films and informative documentaries enlightening me as to how various household gadgets are designed and manufactured. Whilst it is lovely to have a morning flight it is slightly disconcerting to know that when we arrived at our destination we would in fact be re-living the same day again.

We touched down at O'Hare International Airport after a flawless flight and asked directions to the 'L' train to take us to downtown. What always strikes me as I leave the airport is just how polite everyone is. I see none of the indifference or reserve one may experience when asking directions in a European city. In fact, the last time I asked for directions in London I had to abandon my quest for the simple reason that I couldn't find anybody that wasn't a tourist. One of my children recently exhibited an interest in hearing a real life Australian accent and I was obliged to reply with "just go to London and ask for directions".

After asking an unnecessary number of passers-by for help just to hear their accents and be complimented on mine, we proceeded to the train station.

At the risk of being a little contentious, I am inclined to say that like so many nationalities, the Americans are definitely at their best on home turf. As a European who is regularly fed a media diet of violent atrocities from across the pond, I half expected to be gunned down at customs. My experiences, fortuitous for anybody taking the trouble to read this book, have been to the contrary. To date, all my dealings with Americans have been friendly and courteous. I find the vast majority always willing to go that extra mile to make my stay there more enjoyable. Ok, it is true that I have only really come into contact with people either in the hospitality industry, or used to being in regular contact with bewildered tourists, but I am a great believer in credit where credit is due!

A few minutes later we were trundling towards the cluster of skyscrapers that dominate downtown Chicago.

Having always travelled business class, my brother seemed unfamiliar with the concept of walking to ones destination and was all for getting a taxi to the hotel. I, on the other hand, being a legendary tight-arse like to make use of 'Shank's pony' whenever I can. I somewhat smugly advocate the obvious health benefits, making light of the fact that I get to hold on to my precious dollars for a bit longer.

Unfortunately our first walk through the streets of downtown were slight soured when the wheel fell off of my brothers wheelie-case, resulting in him having to carry his heavy luggage the five remaining blocks to the hotel. By the time we got there my suave, executive brother looked more like a sweaty porter and I had to come to terms with the fact that all my future suggestions would more than likely be greeted with contempt.

# *Six*

After checking into our hotel, the others settled down for a siesta whilst I took the opportunity to brush up on my Chicago history.

Originally home to the native Potawatomi Indians, the first recorded European settlers didn't arrive until the late 1700's and consisted mainly of French fur traders, explorers and missionaries. The word *Chicago* evolved when the French tried, not very successfully, to pronounce the name of a plant known locally as *shikaakwa*, ubiquitous along the Chicago River. After many scuffles between the natives and the speech impeded settlers over land rights, the modern city of Chicago was founded in the 1830's, with a population of less than four thousand.

The opening of the Illinois and Michigan canal in 1848, allowed shipping to pass freely all the way from the Great Lakes to the Mississippi and on to the Gulf of Mexico. Chicago was conveniently placed along the route and this, combined with the arrival of the railroad, cemented the city's reputation as transportation hub.

By 1870, the city's population had reached 300,000, largely boosted by European settlers. A year later it was ravaged by fire, aided by the prevalence of timber constructions built in close proximity to one another (you'd think they may have learned a lesson from 1666's London). The new city was almost totally destroyed.

After this catastrophe, a stringent new fire safety code was introduced, not surprisingly giving preference to masonry constructions. The new legislation brought with it new challenges, as the soft, lakeside ground was mostly unsuitable for the heavier buildings. In order to overcome this, a revolutionary way of using steel as a supporting framework was developed. This, coupled with new technical innovations such as lifts, fire-proofing and telecommunications led to the age of the skyscraper. An unprecedented amount of growth followed as the city gathered momentum creating employment and wealth.

However, the state of law and order left a lot to be desired. By the 1900's the city had reached worldwide notoriety for its impressive murder rates. The justice system often failed to convict murderers even if their identities were known. Organised crime flourished throughout the years of prohibition during the 1920's, as bootleggers smuggled in vast quantities of alcohol from neighboring Canada. Profits were huge and criminals such as Al Capone were glamorised by the media. However, the city's sinister reputation didn't seem to deter anybody. Throughout the century immigrants from all over the world continued to flock there in search of a better life, thus creating the cosmopolitan melting pot it is today.

For our first excursion on foot we decided to walk down to Lake Michigan to get our bearings. Looking back, the skyline is dominated by what was, for many years of my life, the tallest building in the world, known then as the Sears Tower but currently known as the Willis Tower. With no other immediate plan, this was our chance to check it out, so without further ado, we turned on our heels and headed inland. It was further away than it looked but fuelled by a quick coffee stop we made it in under an hour.

After a short wait for tickets, we ascended the 103 floors in the super fast lift to the skydeck and took in the stunning views of the vast metropolis which is Chicago. The architects of this wonderful building decided to take the sight-seeing experience one step further. Partly inspired by the scene in the film *Ferris Bueller's Day Off*, when a group of adolescents push their faces up against the glass to try and get the full height experience, they added 'The Ledge'. There are four solid glass balconies, built with the sole purpose of scaring the wits out of us vertigo sufferers. As I waited anxiously for my turn, a member of staff informed us that the glass was three inches thick, could withstand five tons in weight and was indeed "unbreakable". The kind gentleman behind me responded by telling me about an incident in 2009 when a family entered onto the balcony to take photos and the glass floor appeared to shatter beneath them. They were assured by staff afterwards (information that I imagine came too late to save their underwear) that it was only a protective coat of glass that had disintegrated and that there had been no danger of them tumbling 412 meters to be greeted by the pavement and eternal rest.

So with this in mind I gingerly ventured out over the nothingness for what felt like a good five minutes (but was about the equivalent in seconds), just to confirm that "yep, everything did indeed look tiny down there". Considering that part of the journey done, I then decided to take a look at the museum display while my testicles dropped back into their rightful place.

On completion in 1973, the tower surpassed the twin towers in New York to become the tallest building in the world. At the heady height of 442 meters it reigned supreme for nearly 25 years and is still, according to the Willis Group, the tallest building in North America. It all depends on how the height is calculated, i.e. does it include antennas, number of inhabited floors etc - it seems to be a very contentious subject and so I'll leave it at that. Apparently on a clear day one can see the four states of

Wisconsin, Michigan, Illinois and Indiana. I'm afraid I cannot vouch for that but I can verify that the views are spectacular.

After a super fast descent we all needed a drink and, as luck would have it, we stumbled across an Irish pub. Seemingly omnipresent around the globe, the Irish pub typifies the same reassuring familiarity to those of us partial to a pint as I'm sure McDonald's does to those in search of a clean toilet. We walked down some stairs, leading off of a quiet street and entered into a bustling haven of conviviality, serenaded by the dulcet tones of Axl Rose and the heartening clip of cue-on-ball. We sat at the bar and chatted to the uncharacteristically grumpy, but none-the-less entertaining barman, eating cheesey nachos and sampling the selection of local brews. He turned out to be a mine of information and informed us amongst other things that, unlike the rest of the world, Chicagoan's never referred to their town as 'the windy city'; apparently every St Patrick's day is celebrated by dyeing the Chicago River green; locals use the rather unusual local custom of "dibs" to overcome parking disputes during the winter months.

Apparently Chicago residents prefer to drive during the freezing winter months rather than using public transport, even when the cars are literally buried in snow. It has long been considered that anyone who expends energy digging snow off of their car has a certain right to that parking space. In order to have "dibs" on the space they leave amongst other things, items of garden furniture in the road to reserve what they consider to be their spot. Although the custom is honored by city officials to a point, it isn't foolproof and there have been many heated disputes over parking rights, often ending with vehicles damaged or even blown up with explosives.

Having been suitably enlightened with Chicagoan factoids and with several new beers added to my brothers list, we staggered out into what was now the evening on a mission to track down the famous Chicago deep pan pizza.

Our friendly barman, who was incidentally about as Irish as I am, had recommended a pizzeria close to our hotel by the name of Giordano's Pizza House. It was easy to find and after a short wait and another (enormous) beer, I ordered the 'classic deep pan', a house specialty promising an abundance of fresh sausage, pepperoni, mushrooms and extra cheese. Delicious but hugely oversized for my meager European appetite, I managed to eat a third of it, thriftily taking the rest home for the following day's lunch.

By now jet lag was kicking in so we retired to our hotel full of anticipation (and pizza) for the three weeks ahead.

# *Seven*

Sharing a room (I feel the urge to clarify room *not* bed) with two guys is usually quite an unpleasant experience due to the likelihood of proliferate flatulence and the very real possibility of happening upon a snorer. Being a light sleeper I have a tendency to become anxious in unknown situations but as it turned out, my travel buddies were impeccably behaved and we all slept well.

Due to the jetlag, we were all wide awake by five o'clock in the morning so as breakfast was not included in our hotel, we strolled across town, crossing the Chicago River to find Eggy's Diner. Looking to experience the quintessential American diner breakfast, we were informed that this was the place to go and we were not disappointed. I chose the *Eggy's Combo* , consisting of two eggs, two pancakes, two strips of bacon and two sausage links  (I'm salivating on my laptop as I write) washed down with a bottomless cup of coffee - for me a near perfect start to the day.

Feeling re-energised we strolled down to the impressive Navy Pier.

Completed in 1916 it was heralded as the world's largest pier, built to handle the expanding shipping industry of Lake Michigan. It quickly became popular as a place for public gatherings and by popular demand a theatre and picnic area was added. Present day attractions include a rather large Ferris wheel, a museum, sculptures, restaurants and boutiques.

After a brief spell of souvenir hunting we arrived at the booth selling tickets for various river cruises. Whilst I championed a boat ride on Lake Michigan to take photos of the skyline, my brother and Alex were insistent that we should take the less reasonably priced 'Architectural River Cruise'. After a rather intense key side discussion throwing around words like 'budget' and 'bollocks', I caved in and we made our purchase.

We proceeded to the docks at Polk Bros Park to find our boat. We were first to arrive and after carefully selecting what we thought might be the best seats, we waited patiently in the sunshine as a steady stream of fellow tourists trickled on board. Our guide introduced himself as an architectural student by the name of Brad or Chad (sorry I didn't catch his name) and as we cast off he started what was an impressive and informative seventy-five minute discourse, seemingly without taking a breath. As we cruised up the Chicago River, under bridges, past historic sites and breathtaking skyscrapers we were bombarded with information at almost amphetamine speed.

One of the most notable buildings from a personal stance was the Merchandise Mart. Located close to the river on Chicago's North side, the building opened for business in 1930, centralizing the city's wholesale goods market under one roof. It was the largest building in the world providing 372,000 square meters of floor space, and before you ask, I have no idea on what criteria they choose the largest building but I know it has nothing to do with antenna! The building is so humungous that up until 2008 it had its own zip code. It was owned by the Kennedy family for some 50 years and is reputedly valued at a staggering one billion dollars in today's real-estate market. We passed the Trump International Hotel and Tower which, during its years of conception, was planned to become the tallest building in the world. Unfortunately after the 9/11 attacks, the designers sensibly decided on a more modest version. The resulting construction, completed in 2009, achieved 423 meters in height and reigned as the building with the highest residential apartments until the completion of the Burj Khalifa.

With instruction from our guide all heads turned towards the Field Building or Bank of America Building which now stands on the site of what was arguably considered the world's first skyscraper, the Home

Insurance Building. Opened in 1884, this ten story structure was built using a steel framework to drastically reduce its weight, making it two thirds lighter than a traditional masonry construction. The weight reduction meant that the building could be taller and two more floors were added in 1890. Unfortunately this ill-fated skyscraper was demolished a few years later to make way for taller, shinier architecture.

Two of the most striking riverside structures are collectively known as Marina City. Upon completion in 1964, the sixty-five story towers were the tallest residential constructions in the world, inspired presumably by somebody sticking a couple of maize cobs into the ground. The complex apparently contains everything one needs to enjoy life including shops, restaurants, swimming pool, gym, bowling alley, ice rink and a marina.

In my experience there aren't many tourist excursions that offer true value for money, but I feel compelled to say that, as we walked off the gang plank, we all had the same impression that we had 'connected' with this fascinating city.

We strolled up and down the River Walk and then on to the Ohio Street Beach for a paddle in the September sunshine. Some menacingly dark clouds appeared on the horizon, signifying a coming storm blowing in from the lake, so we turned on our heels and made for the hotel. Before we had reached the end of the block the storm was upon us. Aggressive gusts of wind whipped up dust and leaves and pelted our eyes making it hard to walk straight, shortly followed by rain drops the size of paint balls. To avoid a drenching, we ducked into the nearest building which happened to be the *Museum of Contempory Art.*

I wandered around content to be out of torrential rain but slightly embarrassed by my inability to connect with the majority of exhibits. It's true that I've never studied pop art or contemporary art, but I've never studied music or tennis either, and yet I still manage to enjoy them. I much prefer more obvious art and preferably the kind that involves a high degree of skill on the artists part. Give me a good Canaletto landscape or perhaps a sculpture by Michael Angelo and I can stare at it for several minutes marveling at the detail and the prodigious talent involved in its creation. But to be in a room with something that has to have its very reason for being labeled as 'art' explained to me, leaves me feeling inadequate and quite frankly bored. All this piffle about challenging ones perceptions of art – as far as I know, my perceptions are quite content to be left unchallenged in a world where a very limited understanding of the subject  leaves me blissfully unaware of any subliminal meaning that the artist may or may not have intended.

All I'm trying to say is that to stick something in a gallery and call it art isn't enough. To me art has to be beautiful, awe-inspiring, creative and well executed. Not some old tat or accident on a page that often ends up in so called contemporary art museums. In a situation reminiscent of *The Emperor's New Clothes*, the real winners are obviously the artists who must be laughing at us all the way to the bank. However, the building is lovely, the staff were friendly, the cafeteria was great and the toilets were nice and clean but then again I could say the same about Ikea.

The storm was over as quickly as it began, so we headed back to our lodgings to chill out, call home and talk about the evening. As we only had one night left in the city and so many places to choose from it was necessary to select carefully to ensure the best possible 'blues' experience. My brother was pushing for a visit to 'Buddy Guy's Legends' whilst Alex was keen on the 'Kingston Mines', a bar highly recommended by a friend. We decided to go with what was to us the lesser known Kingston Mines in the hope of a more earthly, less touristy experience.

Situated a few minutes by train on the north side of Chicago, I must admit that even after our warm reception I was slightly unnerved by the prospect of visiting an unknown suburb in a city that was once the murder capital of the USA. My fears were quickly allayed however during the short walk from the train station to the bar. No sign of any black Cadillac's with tinted windows or gangs hanging on street corners, just leafy avenues and unthreatening looking locals going about their business. We arrived as the bar opened, settling in for a beer and chatting to the friendly buxom barmaid. In a matter of minutes the room filled up with blues fans, seemingly from all over the world and the atmosphere became relaxed and friendly. We chatted to a group of ladies from Australia each sporting matching fur hats (I never did ask why), trading travel experiences as the first band set up their instruments. I was slightly disappointed to see no semi-acoustic Gibson guitar up on stage as to me the instrument is synonymous with the blues, but hey, give the poor guys a chance!

The lights dimmed and the music started and we were blown away with the quality of the vocal harmonies and musicianship. A few songs into the set, the front man ventured out into the crowd and pulled people out of their comfort zones and on to the dance floor. Leaving my English reserve in the bottom of one of the many empty beer bottles, I followed suit. What followed was what I believe to be a fairly impressive display of my entire repertoire of dance moves. Two minutes later I sat down with my companions waiting for some kind of compliment, only to be rather unfairly compared to a man slipping repeatedly on the same patch of ice.

The first set finished and it was then that I noticed something that to me seemed fairly unique. There was a second stage in a room next door with a band set up and ready play. The 'Kinston Mines' experience consisted of virtually not stop music, as the audience passed back and forth from band to band. I was comforted to see that the guitarist in the second band had chosen what I slightly pretentiously considered to be the right guitar (Gibson ES 335) and as the music started we floated up to 'blues heaven' and remained there for the rest of the night. After my brother had bought several of the band's signed CD's we said farewell to the barmaid, who stared at us rather intently and gave us the parting words "make the right decisions boys". She probably says this to everybody, but to three semi-inebriated, jet lagged blokes from England at the beginning of a long journey, those enigmatic words mildly freaked us out. Why could she not have said "yep, cheers lads, have a good one" like any self-respecting landlord/lady. What was she talking about? Did she know something that we didn't? Was this whole thing some sort of celestial test? Those questions and more like them hung in the air on the 'L' train ride back to our stop but were quickly forgotten during a mandatory fast food stop. Feeling secure even in the dead of night, we stumbled back to the hotel for a well-earned sleep.

# *Eight*

Looking in the mirror to be greeted with an unkempt slob staring back at me, I made the brave decision to face the razor that morning. Normally preferring to use an electric shaver, I am no friend of the rather more dangerous manual version. No matter which make of razor I buy or how much the manufacturer promises a painless shave, I always end up slashing my face and bleeding profusely on all and sundry.

On that particular morning I felt confident that a tube of super-duper-sensitive-no-blood-guaranteed shaving gel that I found in our bathroom drawer (secretly rejoicing that that was one less pre-trip purchase), was going to make the experience pain free. After spreading a copious amount over my lower visage, unknowingly forming a large puddle on the bathroom floor as the tube split, I detected a distinct odour of what I can only liken to a mixture of goat's cheese and stale washing. Checking the packaging to find the product advertised as mildly perfumed I then checked the sell by date which recorded manufacture in the previous decade. Having already shaved a small portion of my face I deemed it necessary to continue as best as I could with the rotten slime and five minutes later I exited the bathroom as usual, looking like I'd put my head through the bathroom mirror.

We checked out of our hotel and following my brothers steadfast refusal to walk with our bags, took a taxi to the new eastside to the hire car depot where we were introduced to what was to be our 'wheels' for the long haul to Miami. After much deliberation my brother had chosen a Dodge Enclave. A mid-sized SUV that was really too big for the three of us, but would be useful during the second half of the trip when we would be joined by Neil.

After getting accustomed to the onboard equipment it became apparent that we had no GPS, so I took it upon myself to run maniacally around the streets of Chicago in search of a road map. Five shops later I found what I was looking for and we mounted up and rode out of town.

The car was well designed and luxurious compared to what I'm used to and definitely solid enough to make one feel secure. Heading out on interstate 55 we followed the historic Route 66 made famous by the legendary *Chuck Berry*.

After a while the conversation lulled and I tried to recall details of my previous visit to the area. I remembered trundling towards Chicago all those years ago on my way home to say goodbye to a beloved Grandmother, surprised by the sheer barrenness of this area. I had been staying with a friend and his Bible bashing family in Iowa, a period that I don't remember a great deal about other than a conversation with his father concerning my future.

On the day of my arrival he asked me some well rehearsed questions that I suppose constituted some form of psycho-analysis. I presumed he quite rightly needed to gauge my character before letting me stay in his house or hang out with his son. "Boy", he said, "do you own a Bible?" to which I honestly answered "No". His thought process was palpable  and after a bit of beard scratching he fired the second question at me..."Boy", do you believe that the Lord Jesus Christ, is our savior?". I'm afraid I had to answer negatively for a second time, news that he rather worryingly took like a physical blow. After several seconds of silence he rather apologetically announced that I was going to burn in eternal hell and damnation.

I did stay there a couple of nights and their hospitality was excellent in true American style but as you can imagine we didn't particularly warm to each other after that.

Once we had left the suburbs there was not really a great deal of interest to look at and so we contented ourselves with our various road trip playlists and ploughed on towards Springfield.

Having not eaten or drunk yet I was becoming increasingly more bad tempered by the minute so we agreed to stop at a roadside diner for some sustenance. Our waitress was Sandy and she was ideally suited to her job. She took our orders and brought us food and coffee with remarkable efficiency, all the time making the kind of warm conversation that makes one feel like a valued customer.

It crossed my mind that if I should ever end up a sad, lonely old git, I will buy a house next to one of these friendly diners and challenge the staff to lift my spirits on a regular basis. Although judging by the delicious plate of fatty calories we were served up, they wouldn't have to suffer me for very long.  After an unsuccessful attempt to contact home (although frustrating at the time, it is refreshing to know that even in the land of the internet, the wifi can be crap), we popped next door to the local Target to stock up on fruit. It's amazing how interspersing the burgers and beer with the odd apple or pear eases ones conscience considerably. This achieved we continued our journey, arriving at our destination mid-afternoon.

As we passed through the clapboard houses towards the town centre my first impression of Springfield was that it appeared clean and charming. Quickly familiarizing ourselves with the grid layout, it was easy to locate the Lincoln Home Visitors Centre. We found a convenient parking space and gasped as we opened the car doors. The Illinois heat was stifling and it made me reflect on whether we were witnessing the effects of global warming or just another freak heat wave.

We perused the visitors centre and discovered that there is a lot to see here, including the Presidential Museum, a replica of the town that Lincoln lived in and his tomb at the Oak Ridge cemetery.

The town was originally called Calhoun after a senator of the same name but in 1832 when he fell out of favour, the search was on for a new name. At this time there happened to be a town by the name of Springfield in Massachusetts which was doing rather well. This town had become prosperous by manufacturing firearms for the U.S. military, using the then state-of-the-art technique of assembly lines to mass produce. Calhoun wanted to mimic the success of this progressive town and so it took the name Springfield and never looked back. It became the capital city of Illinois in 1839, largely due to lobbying by Lincoln and his friends who were known as the Long Nine, due to their unusual height. Rather bizarrely, he and the eight other men that formed the Illinois general counsel at that time were all over six feet tall. Lincoln himself measured in at a lanky six feet and four inches, making him the tallest U.S. president to date.

Today, although having one of the most common toponyms in the USA (apparently appearing in at least 34 states), it is the only Springfield that can refer to itself as a state capital.

We made our way through the park brandishing our cameras, making full use of an unexpected photo opportunity, in the form of a life-sized bronze of Abraham Lincoln sitting on a park bench. We took it in turns to sit next to him, as I'm sure every visitor does, trying not to burn our posteriors on the baking metal.

Lincoln arrived here as a young man and worked for twenty four years as a practicing lawyer. He then moved on to the Whitehouse and guided the country through the terrible civil war and the abolition of slavery. This remarkable man's life was cut short by a bullet in the head, fired at point blank range by a confederate spy during a theatre performance in 1865.

There are reminders that this is the land of Lincoln everywhere and given the chance I would have willingly perused the many museums and historic sites but alas, we had nowhere near enough time to do it justice. I guess I'll just have to come back one day.

We wandered down the majestic Capital Avenue as far as the magnificent domed Capital Complex. In more recent history, it was in the grounds of these beautiful buildings that the then Senator Barack Obama announced his presidential candidacy in 2007.

By now we were suffering a little in the heat, so we ducked into an air-conditioned bar for a little respite and a glass of something cold. With evening fast approaching, we made the decision to look for accommodation for the night. Our friendly bar girl managed to recount her entire life story to us which thankfully, due to her young age didn't take very long. She recommended a hotel across the road and so we decided to check it out. They had no three bed rooms, so I shared a twin with Alex and my brother had to go it alone.

Having underestimated the September weather my first task upon dumping our luggage was to find a shop and get some sunglasses and sandals. We drove out through some less salubrious looking suburbs to the nearest Wal-Mart and rubbed shoulders with the kind of people one is rarely exposed to in the televised version of America. That is unless you watch something along the lines of *Half Ton Mum* or *Tattoos Gone Wrong*.

We found what we needed at a very reasonable price and headed back to the car, trying not to make eye contact with anyone on route.

We dropped the car off at the hotel and ventured into downtown on what was an exquisite summer evening, passing over an unusual number of train tracks along the way. It was evident that when the railroad arrived here, the town became a major transportation hub. I couldn't begin to imagine the everyday noise, steam, hustle and bustle and excitement when these lines were in full use. On this particular evening it was even harder to imagine as the town seemed deserted.

As luck would have it we happened upon the *Craft Beer Bar* and it now became obvious that the streets were empty because everybody was here drinking an amicable potation after a hard day at the office. Nope; we entered hoping to find atmosphere akin to an English city pub, but it very quickly became apparent that it was just us and a very bored looking bar lady. Before us there were two hundred different beers to choose from, including fourteen on draught. As the barmaid roused herself from her semi-coma and asked for our orders I could see my brother was thoroughly discombobulated by this vast selection and for a moment he was at a loss for words. Many of the names were very intriguing, such as *Half Acre Daisy Cutter, Smuttynose Rocky Road,* and *Peppermint Victory at Sea* but sadly we couldn't try them all. I contented myself with *a Big Muddy Pumpkin Smasher,* followed by a *Dogfish Head Beer To Drink Music To* at which point we decided to leave, resisting a charitable urge to keep the poor lady company in her beery dungeon. Still optimistic of finding some sign of life, we searched for somewhere to eat but there didn't seem to be a lot of choice. Wandering a block or two further on we witnessed some rough edges to this otherwise pristine town. As in many towns, the homeless community tends to appear in force after dark. I remember once during a long weekend in Paris, having to set my alarm for four o'clock in the morning to top up the parking meter, in order to prevent my car from being towed away. As I walked towards my car, the street was alive with homeless people, delving through bins and shivering under piles of old rags. Where these people go during the day is a mystery to me but I guess they are less hassled by the police at night and can continue their pitiful existence comparatively unhindered. The vagrants of Springfield were not shy and retiring and seemed to be having a better evening than we were, sipping and passing around their bottles of moonshine or whatever it is they drink now. They had their obligatory savage looking dogs with them and feeling a little threatened we ducked into the nearest restaurant. It happened to serve Italian cuisine and went by the name of *Mangia* which apparently means 'eats' in Italian. As soon as I walked in I liked the place with its exposed brick and black and white photos of Frank Sinatra and Dean Martin. We were shown to a table right at the back of the restaurant by a quirky, punk rock styled waitress, that judging by her spunky nature, definitely had some Italian blood from somewhere down the line. I ordered sea food pasta and it arrived quickly and tasted delicious. The portions were copious so we made the bold decision to skip dessert and headed back towards our hotel, still hoping to find some entertainment but, apart from the hobos, everywhere seemed deserted. I guess that like many capital cities, when the working day is done, everyone goes back to suburbia to see their wife and kids and who can blame them?

# *Nine*

We awoke to a motel breakfast of biscuits and gravy which we bravely tried but couldn't actually swallow on account of it tasting like shit. We were informed by the waitress that this was apparently a Southern treat, consisting of what an Englishman would call scones, covered in gravy made from pig fat. Apparently the meal emerged when food was in short supply for the early settlers and has become (just like frogs and snails in France) a bit of a delicacy. I'd like to flatter myself as quite a daring eater but I'm afraid to say that, along with its French equivalents, this thrifty meal-come-delicacy didn't appeal to my Anglo-Saxon palate.

After a quick burger and a Skype home in the suburbs we rejoined the historic Route 66, following directions to St. Louis.

Our schedule necessitated arriving in Nashville the following day so we made the decision to drive through St. Louis without stopping, just to catch a glimpse of the skyline with its famous arch and the mighty Mississippi river.

Before crossing into Missouri we had to pass through East St. Louis, a smaller city with the rather dubious reputation of having one of the highest crime rates in the U.S. We slowed down to try to get a glimpse of the Gateway Geyser, a 192 meter fountain built to rival St. Louis Arch. Apparently the second tallest of its kind in the world, it ejaculates three times a day, but unfortunately for us our timing was not so good and we missed the show.

I gunned the car across the bridge, traversing the celebrated muddy waters of the Mississippi river below. The arch was upon us all at once and, with windows down and all hands on cameras in a frenzy of photography, we miraculously made it to Missouri still intact.

Designed by Finnish American architect Eero Saarinen and completed in 1965, the Gateway Arch towers above the city, climbing to a height of 192 meters. This remarkable stainless steel clad structure holds the illustrious title of *the world's tallest arch* and has become the internationally famous symbol of St. Louis. It is so humungous that it even incorporates a tram system; transporting sightseers to the observation deck to enjoy what I imagine must be stunning views.   Not everyone agreed with Saararin when he named the arch *The Gateway to the West*. The Kansas born poet Calvin Trillin wrote,

"I know you're thinking that there are considerable differences between T.S. Eliot and me. Yes, it is true that he was from St Louis, which started calling itself the Gateway to the West after Eero Saarinen's  Gateway Arch was erected, and I'm from Kansas City, where people think of St. Louis not as the Gateway to the West but as the Exit from the East."

Content with some memorable photos of our deviation into St. Louis, we exited on Route 55, direction Tennessee.

We were making good progress but the plan was not to arrive in Nashville until the following day. After a brief look at the map the decision was made to break our journey at a town called Paducah, for no other reason than that we liked the name.

Trundling across the state line into Kentucky there were no apparent changes in the surroundings, but we were now entering into the famous "Dixieland".

In fact the word "Dixie" originates from the banks of New Orleans who printed their own currency back in the days before the Louisiana Purchase. The ten dollar bills known as "dix" by the French became known as "Dixies" by the English speaking Southerners.

Shortly after entering Tennessee we were heading towards downtown Paducah. Parking up we strolled into the visitor's centre and were warmly greeted by two lovely ladies. They indulged us with many questions about our backgrounds (I'm pretty sure that they presumed that we were gay) and how we had happened upon their little town. They turned out to be highly efficient at their jobs and within minutes we had a stack of fascinating leaflets, a town badge each, and an appointment to view a rental apartment across the road. After inspecting the property, which was indeed fabulous but unfortunately out of our budget, the lovely ladies called and booked us a hotel on the edge of town. With not many hours of day light left it was time to search for adventure.

The town is located on the confluence of the Tennessee and Ohio River and owes much of its original prosperity to locomotive workshops and its location as a river port.

Walking down towards the historic river front we passed a large paneled wall which was described on one of our leaflets as a flood barrier. In every panel a mural had been painstakingly painted, each depicting a scene from the town's history. There are over fifty paintings illustrating a wide variety of subjects, including Native Americans, locomotives, notable local buildings, street scenes and riverboats, all expertly designed and executed by the artist Robert Dafford.

After studying the wall for several minutes we passed through an opening and enjoyed some stunning views of the river. I am always slightly envious of those lucky enough to reside in a town on the banks of a major confluence. Aside from the obvious flooding potential, there is something incredibly therapeutic about sitting at the water's edge and observing the river life, both natural and manmade. Paducah was no exception. With a view like this there is no need for a cathedral or church to meditate on life's enigmas. Just to fix one's eyes on the horizon would be enough therapy for most people, I'm sure. I could have sat in this spot for hours but alas, the need for sustenance was beginning to overpower us.

Passing by a beautifully renovated locomotive complete with carriages, we made the most of the photo opportunity and headed down Broadway. The elegant brick clad buildings could have been straight out of a Western and it was easy to image stage coaches running up and down the street. We dived into a friendly looking bar and downed a couple of cold ones but the menu wasn't very appealing. After all the burgers and hot dogs we had consumed, it was definitely time to find something healthier. There were a number of good restaurants in the vicinity so we chose one and ate Moroccan chicken and cous cous whilst chatting to a very talented barman. Looking a bit like Don Johnson with a goatee beard, he informed us that his day jobs included actor, musician and artist. It always strikes me as sad that there are so many creative people in this world and the vast majority seem to end up in the hospitality industry. But on reflection, he entertained us for a while so maybe his talents aren't totally wasted.

We wandered back to the hotel and were pleasantly surprised to find it was 'cookie night'. I have never experienced a cookie night anywhere else so I can only imagine that it is a wholly American concept, but what a great idea. Piles of delicious, freshly baked cookies with a variety of fillings including chocolate, caramel and a host of fruits, washed down with fresh coffee or tea at nine o'clock at night, what's not to like? I made a mental note to either starve myself or buy a new wardrobe in the near future. I half heartedly considered a third option; really getting my money's worth in these 'as much as you can eat' situations and then simply investing in a mobility buggy.

# Ten

As we piled up our breakfast plates with scrambled eggs and toast we were confronted with the very sobering images of the 9/11 disaster, on the many TV screens around the dining room. Could it really have been 14 years ago that I had an unexplainable impulse to turn the television on in the middle of a working day, just seconds before the second plane struck? It's moments like that, that really reinforce ones belief in a sixth sense. We sat and watched, still in disbelief at the now familiar scenes of panic stricken people and heroic firefighters emerging from the clouds of dust and ash. I have only been to New York twice. Once in 1990, when I had the good fortune to admire the spectacular scenery from the view deck of the twin towers and take what are now, somewhat unique photos; and last year when I stood at the memorial looking up into the empty sky where I had once stood all those years before. I can only say that I am very thankful that I don't live or work anywhere near a skyscraper.

We checked out of the hotel in a somewhat somber mood, but the anticipation of setting eyes on Nashville for the first time lifted our spirits.

Deciding to take the scenic route, we headed out on another planned detour, an area on the map unimaginatively named *Land Between the Lakes National Reserve*. Although it looked quite appealing on paper, conjuring up mental images of bears and wild elk, the reality was that, from the road, there was very little to be seen. Instead we contented ourselves by observing a succession of small towns with quaint clapboard houses, wooden decks and rocking chairs. We had stumbled across *small town USA*, the inspiration for so many of the songs I love.

As we counted down the miles to Nashville I could feel myself getting excited, something that doesn't happen nearly often enough in the so called *middle* age. Although something I wouldn't necessarily have chosen to admit when I resided in England, I am, along with several members of my family, a fan of country music. I have never really understood why, during my youth, confessing to like country music usually resulted in a brief but harsh period of character assassination. After all, the English champion virtually everything else that is proffered to us from across the pond. I didn't notice many objections to Mc Donald's or Coke or that lovely rap music, so abundant with rhyming profanities that children love to recite. And yet some of the biggest selling musical artists rest relatively unknown in our country as a result of specializing in country music.

I understand that being an adolescent during the punk rock years of the 1970's in England made it hard to relate to songs about pickup trucks and dirt roads. I was first introduced to the genre by the Eagles and Jackson Brown, attracted by the quality of the songs adorned with stunning guitar licks and vocal harmonies. I loved the way the songs usually told a story, sometimes with an element of humour and frequently with a moral message. This formula, along with talent and good looks, has turned singers like Garth Brooks and Taylor Swift into megastars. I took it upon myself to try to educate my brother and Alex, putting on a variety of songs covering subject such as living in a small town, chewing tobacco, lover's revenge and being an outlaw. Not even Brad Paisley and Florida-Georgia Line could win them over. It was all to no avail so I gave up in the end and when my brother put on some more Johnny Cash, I took the opportunity to doze off for a few minutes. Ok, I know that Johnny is a country singer but I'm afraid that for me he represents the old school of classic country that, try as I may, I just don't appreciate.

A little way from the city on the Interstate 24 we stopped for coffee and free wifi at Clarksville, with the intention of booking somewhere to stay. As I approached the counter little did I know that this would be my first encounter with the language barrier. It didn't bode well when I noticed all the employees in a tight bunch, giggling by the shake machine, a scenario rarely encountered in the well-greased cogs of the American fast food chains. After several moments a young girl broke from the pack and drawled in my direction "whaat cn I do fer y'all tday?" The thought entered my head that if she really was in an obliging mood maybe she could give our car a quick clean, but I actually said "I'd like two lattes and a normal coffee please". Looking thoroughly bamboozled, her response was "srrr I dinot unerstaain a werr you saiyd". To which I could only reply "pardon?" Eventually we managed to communicate with a mixture of hand signals and diagrams and successfully carried away our hot beverages, taking shelter in a booth and reminiscing about similar conversations in Glasgow.

The three of us sat there staring at our phones and enjoying the wifi. Incidentally if I had been with my children I'm pretty certain that I would have been chastising them and asking them to put their phones down.....oh the injustice and hypocrisy of it all!

Eventually we got down to the important business of finding accommodation in Nashville. Hoping to find something in the downtown area it soon became obvious that we were out of luck. Everything in and around our budget was booked solid and so with no option available we had to make do with a motel on the edge of town, which had the rather dubious distinction of being judged as 'terrible' sixty-seven times on *Tripadvisor*.

The approach to Nashville was dramatised by an incoming storm, complete with spectacular lightning show and hail storm. Passing by impressive views of the downtown skyline, my first impression was of an opulent, modern city which I'm sure has a lot to do with the music industry.

Our accommodation was near the airport and, contrary to my brother's expectations, for the price it was very agreeable. Our apartment sported two bedrooms, (one missing a door), a very tired kitchen and a bathroom complete with mouldy shower curtain, all very nineteen seventies, circa *Starsky and Hutch.* The complex did have a pool, although the diminishing temperatures after the storm made it slightly less attractive. The most useful service on offer by far was a shuttle bus, departing hourly from reception to downtown and running until the early hours of the morning.

After a brief spell attempting to make ourselves look like cowboys; Alex with his denim shirt and jeans; my brother sporting a shirt that a ranch hand might have worn on a night out and me with my leather boots and Wranglers, we went down to the motel reception to catch the next shuttle bus.

The bus driver dropped us at the river front with directions to find Broadway which, he informed us, is where the action is. A short walk later and we unexpectedly stumbled on what must be one of the great party streets of the world.

I must point out that it was now mid-afternoon on a Thursday, not an hour usually associated with the letting down of one's hair. What confronted us were seemingly wall-to-wall bars, all with live music, a veritable cacophony of sound. Apart from the flashing neon and crowds of fun-seekers hanging over balconies and laughing raucously, the street was filled with what was to me a new concept; *party bikes*. The party bike consisted of a rectangular bar for up to sixteen people with a space in the middle for a bar tender. The whole thing is mounted on wheels with each participant having a set of peddles at their feet. As far as I can see the aim is to consume vast quantities of alcohol whilst simultaneously peddling like crazy, and whooping very loudly. They all seemed to be having a tremendous amount of fun, adding to the general ambiance of Broadway and flouting the drink driving laws in the process.

Starting at one end of the line of neon we worked our way down the street stopping periodically for beer. The quality of musicianship was excellent and as afternoon turned to evening the music changed from traditional country to rock, which suited me down to the ground.

One of the bars doubled up as a boot shop by day and after several tankards of the local brew it took all my willpower not to invest in a pair of bright red, snakeskin boots. It was sensibly pointed out to me that one would have to be nothing short of feminine to pull them off in Europe. A few beers more, strategically mixed with burgers and hot dogs, and we were rapidly approaching the 'good for nothing' segment of the evening. It was time to stumble back to the riverfront feeling as if we had given Broadway a good run.

The shuttle bus experience had changed considerably from our subdued inward voyage. The bus was teaming with well liquored cowboys in their ten gallon hats and cowgirls in denims and cowboy boots. Standing in the aisle of the overcrowded bus, we were inadvertently drawn into a rather one sided dispute between a couple of newly-weds. The rather drunk young man was broadcasting what he considered to be his new wife's imperfections at the top of his voice to all and sundry. My brother carelessly made eye contact with him and from then on became the straight man for a string of chauvinistic one-liners. Even in my drunken state I could tell that some very large cowboys were getting ready to step in and defend the poor women's honour. I was greatly relieved when the shuttle reached our stop and we retired to the peaceful motel room.

Unlike our relatively firearm free environment in Europe, I am constantly aware that in the USA, any kind of dispute, no matter how trivial, could end up in some unwanted gun play. The statistics are staggering. I read an article in *The Guardian* newspaper recently estimating that there are as many as three hundred million guns here. I'm sure this has something to do with the average American's general tendency to be polite to everyone for fear of deadly reprisals.

Whilst driving we noticed that nobody flashes their headlights or leans on the hooter to express dissatisfaction with other road users. I'm sure that the average Parisian would last about three seconds here before being gunned down for honking at somebody who had the audacity to wait a nanosecond more than necessary when the lights turned to green. Imagine having the hardware to shoot the tires out of that BMW driver that pounces on you the second you pull out to overtake a slow moving vehicle. Virtually touching the rear bumper and flashing the headlights until you are so intimidated that you deviate in a dangerous fashion to let the butthole past. Then, not content with gaining the coveted twenty meters of road between you and the car in front that meant so much to him a second ago, he starts the process of harassment all over again, working his way ineptly down the endless line of cars that frequent British roads. What does he gain by this behavior, I wonder? Three more minutes with his kids before bedtime? Another glass of wine with his loving wife? I suspect it is more like a fleeting sensation of bullying virility in a world otherwise dominated by an over-bearing wife whose sex life has recently been improved ten-fold by the purchase of a plastic aid in preference to hubby's micro-manhood. A bit harsh? I think not. Let's just enjoy the 'shooting out the tyres' moment before boring old rationality kicks in.

# *Eleven*

The motel breakfast consisted of over sweetened everything washed down with 'donkey piss' coffee (as they say in France), however we were not disheartened as today was a big day. We would be visiting the famous *RCA Studio B* and the *Country Music Hall of Fame*.

We took our car into downtown and parked up on 4th Street, walking past vast new developments adorning this modern city. Arriving at the impressive entrance to the *Country Music Hall of Fame and Museum* we were greeted on entry by a Mr. David Anderson. He was standing in the foyer playing his bluegrass and country guitar licks, periodically pausing to welcoming visitors into the building. During a very pleasant conversation, he explained that he worked as an ambassador for country music. He showed us a photo album of himself standing next to many legends of Nashville including Garth Brooks, whom we learned had been inducted into the Country Music Walk of Fame only the day before. That explained why we had trouble finding a room. I was a little disappointed as it would have been great to see him but 'c'est la vie'.

We took several photos of Mr. Anderson, and after giving each of us a souvenir guitar pick, he even let me strum his instrument. We thanked him heartily for his time and went off to collect our tickets for the tour before enjoying a cappuccino and a blueberry muffin on the airy terrace. Finally our tour number was called and we were steered onto the bus by our tour guide, Geoff, to make the short journey to RCA Studio B. Geoff bombarded us with facts and stories concerning the history of the studio, making the ten minute trip very interesting.

The bus pulled up outside a square building, remarkable only due to the presence of a giant replica of Roy Orbison's guitar standing in front of it. As our group entered the building, Geoff filled us in on some of the history.

Located on downtown's *Music Row*, the building was constructed by Dan Maddox in 1957, in response to demands by Chet Atkins and Steve Sholes for a state-of-the-art recording facility. Credited with helping to create the *Nashville Sound,* in the early years the studio team built a reputation for sophisticated backing vocals and string sections which helped to popularise country music. With over a thousand hit records under its belt, the list of artists that have recorded there are impressive indeed; The

Everly Brothers, Willy Nelson, Roy Orbison, Dolly Parton, Johnny Cash and, of course, Elvis Presley to name but a few.

We stood in the lobby surrounded by photos of the artists in their prime and listened to some of the greatest recordings, interspersed with fascinating stories of studio shenanigans. Encouraged by our 'California' confident guide we sang our hearts out, creating a memorable ambiance before finally walking down a short corridor and into the actual studio. The room was fairly large with a glass screen at one end, behind which lay the recording and mixing equipment. The studio itself was fairly sparse, the most obvious thing in the room being the old piano on which so many great artists had played. We were shown the lighting system installed specifically for Elvis and Geoff explained the reasoning behind this rather strange addition.

Suffering from insomnia, Elvis preferred to record during the dark hours and rarely did anything productive before midnight. He had requested the multi-coloured lights as apparently specific colours helped him to get into the mood for the particular style of song that he was recording. On the night they recorded *Lonesome Tonight* he had tried all the variations of lighting but was still unable to get the mood right, so eventually they turned the lights off and he sang in the dark. The resulting recording was the best of the bunch, however at the end of the song unable to see, he inadvertently banged his head on the microphone. As we sat in the studio with the lights off and listened to the original recording, it was like being able to sit in on a session with the great man, and guess what - you can actually hear Elvis hit his head at the end of the recording. With the lights back on we were able to take photos and stand on the spot marked with a cross of blue tape, where Elvis preferred to stand and sing.

As we left the building Geoff showed us the crack in the wall where Dolly Parton, late for a recording session, had arrived too fast one day and drove into the wall. All in all, this visit was for me the unexpected highlight of our time in Nashville.

The bus dropped us back to the main building and we wandered into the museum for a look around. This place is a veritable Mecca for anybody interested in the history of country music. There were special exhibits on Sam Phillips, Johnny Cash and Bob Dylan and so many impressive artifacts that we could not possibly do it justice in an afternoon. We gave it our best shot, pausing to photograph many priceless items donated by country artists, from gold Cadillac's to stage outfits and legendary guitars.

We exited the building and crossed the road to take a look at the *Country Music Walk of Fame*. This consists of a pleasant paved area with inset black marble plaques set into the pavement in the style of the stars in Hollywood

Boulevard. All the big names seem to be there and I noted rather poignantly that Garth Brook's plaque looked understandably very shiny. After taking some photos we strolled down to Broadway to look for souvenirs, curious to see if the party was still going on. It was, but we had other plans for the evening.

After freshening up in our shabby but homely motel room, we drove to the Eastern suburbs in search of *Fran's East Side Bar*, mentioned in an article in *The Guardian* newspaper as one of the "places to go". When we eventually found it, it was not much more than an old, scruffy hut. Entering into the unknown, we experienced that heart-sinking moment as all went quiet and all eyes turned towards us, bearing jaw-dropped expressions and resembling rabbits in headlights. We ordered a beer and the atmosphere relaxed as conversation flowed with the locals at the bar. As is often the case after what seems like a hostile reception, the people were actually incredibly friendly. The atmosphere was definitely more homely than bar-like and I made a mental note that if I ever had the good fortune to live in this wonderful city, this would be my local. My brother was under the impression that the bar had live entertainment and he was rather hoping to see some undiscovered talent, playing their hearts out. However upon enquiring we were informed that this was a karaoke bar and that the entertainment didn't start for another two hours. As one of us had to drive we considered it fairer to abort what would have been a super boozy evening and find somewhere quiet to eat instead. The bar lady recommended the Mexican restaurant *Rosepepper Cantina* situated about a mile away, so before I could say 'one for the road' we were off to find it.

The restaurant was just beginning to fill up and the early evening clientele consisted of mainly young families. With an abundance of neon lights and friendly staff I would challenge anybody to be downhearted in this establishment. We were quickly shown to a table and our attentive waiter had beers on the table at breakneck speed. I marvelled again at the efficiency and amiable countenance of your average American waiter/waitress. Whilst Alex and my brother perused the menu I contemplated the many hours of youth wasted standing in a queue three rows back from the bar in a sweaty London pub, wishing that I had an ample bosom to catch the barman's eye; or an otherwise idyllic afternoon sitting in the sun on the terrace of a quaint French restaurant, ruined by the lackadaisical attitude of a haughty waitress who makes it very apparent to all and sundry that this job is way beneath her. All I can say is that there are two ways to look at it. Either enjoy the interaction with clients in the hope of getting a tip, making their day, getting repeat business and thus securing your financial future, or do us all a favour and get another job where we don't have to see your miserable face.

Our waiter tried to tempt us with a choice of over eighty different varieties of tequila but after the previous night's excesses we politely declined. Instead we shared an enormous plate of taco salad and to follow I chose the Rosepepper special, a spicy chicken enchilada served with beans and rice. The food was copious and delicious, so much so that we skipped dessert and headed back to the motel at a shamefully early hour. I really didn't care as my mind was already contemplating the following day. I didn't want to do anything that might affect our chances of reaching Memphis...

# Twelve

We gave the complimentary sugar coated breakfast a wide birth and parted company with our great value motel. Setting off towards what has become to me, an almost mythical city, I viewed the two-hundred-mile route on the map with trepidation. Will I finally get there this time? I pondered on some of the many things that could possibly stop me; mechanical failure, a road accident, a stray lightning bolt; I quickly scanned the horizon for storm clouds. Not a cloud in sight and as we eased onto Interstate 40 I felt quietly optimistic that today was the day.

The route was heavily wooded for what seemed like much of the journey but we eventually reached a clearing and crossed the wide, pristine Kentucky River, stopping at Parkers Crossroads for a re-fuel.

At the Crossroads Cafe we had the unexpected first experience of fried green tomatoes, the waitress being so kind as to bring us an extra portion. The dish was apparently introduced by Jewish immigrants as, I imagine, a creative way of using up the otherwise inedible, un-ripened tomatoes one is sometimes left with at the end of the season. They are thinly sliced and fried in butter and then covered in a crunchy cornmeal batter before being deep fried. When our waitress presented them to us they looked and smelt delicious, but slightly disappointingly for me the tart taste of the unripe fruit still dominates the overall flavor.

We arrived in Memphis in the early afternoon and asked directions to the apartment block in which we were staying. It turned out to be a new development ideally situated right next to the baseball stadium in the heart of town. This budget-busting accommodation was luxurious in every sense of the word, sporting an abundance of fragile ornaments and plant life in extravagant vases. We even had a washing machine which was, at this stage in the trip, a valuable asset.

My brother was due to meet up with his friends from London, who had flown in the previous day, also on a fiftieth birthday excursion. With Alex in tow he went off to find them and visit the *Stacks Museum of Soul Music* on the edge of Memphis. After waiting my whole adult life to visit Beale Street, my curiosity got the better of me and I opted out of the trip and walked into town.

It never ceases to amaze me the influence that a song lyric can have on one's life. I have visited a number of uninteresting places in my life, on the whimsical pretext of liking a particular song featuring the place name, including Albuquerque (thanks a bunch Prefab Sprout). However walking towards Beale Street, humming the Marc Cohn song *Walking in Memphis*, I was sure that this would not be an anticlimax. Following my tourist map I wandered past the baseball stadium, crossing over the road at the Peabody Hotel and headed up Second Avenue.

My first stop was a historical marker outside the original site of Lansky Brothers (now using the slogan "clothier to the King"). The marker tells us that the shop was founded in 1946 by the Lansky Brothers, Bernard and Guy, using a shrewd $125 investment from their father. Bernard took it upon himself to travel the country in search of weird and wonderful fashion items which were at that time unique in Memphis. The clothes were often of bright and vividly coloured fabrics, appealing to the flamboyant artists of the local music industry, including B.B. King, Carl Perkins, Jerry Lee Lewis and Johnny Cash. But it was a young Elvis Presley who was set to change the fortunes of the Lanskys. Bernard noticed him staring through the window admiring the clothing one day and invited him in to look around. He replied that he didn't have any money but one day, when he became rich, he would buy him out. Bernard replied "Don't buy me out, just buy from me", and from then on Elvis did just that. Lansky Brothers supplied clothing throughout his life but it was the flamboyant suits in the fifties that really caught the imagination of the public and helped forge Elvis's image. I turned and spotted the neon sign advertising B.B. Kings Blues Bar and I knew I had finally got to Beale Street.

My first impression was that it was smaller in size than Broadway in Nashville with a more *used* look, like a well-worn boot. In the mid-afternoon heat some of the buildings were almost shabby, however everybody seemed friendly and the bars looked inviting.

There were a much higher proportion of Afro-Americans frequenting the streets, giving the area a much more authentic *Blues* feel. I walked on a bit further, peering into the bars to get a glimpse of the live musicians. Looking around I could easily imagine a young Elvis watching and mimicking the black musicians of the time, creating the crossover style that made him so famous. Here is a street that has seen generations come and go but has remained constant and true to itself; a melting pot of cultures and music.

After a preliminary stroll up and down I pulled up a chair on a shady terrace, ordered a coffee and read a little history.

After thousands of years of occupation by indigenous tribes, the area was first settled by Europeans in the early nineteenth century. The city was founded in 1819 and named Memphis after the ancient Egyptian capital. It rapidly became a major trading center for cotton, at one point boasting the biggest spot cotton market in the world. Currently with a population of over six hundred thousand it is the second largest city in Tennessee after Nashville.

Today, Memphis is better known to the world for its musical heritage. Several music legends have been born in and around the area, including of course Elvis Presley, Jerry Lee Lewis, Johnny Cash, Robert Johnson, Muddy Waters and B.B. King. Beale Street's musical roots began as early as the late nineteenth century as travelling musicians flocked there to play for the wealthy cotton merchants. *The Orpheum Theatre* was added in 1890 and in 1899 the first recorded black millionaire, Robert Church, bought some land and created the Church Park on the corner of 4th Street and Beale. The park became a place for musicians to perform, drawing crowds and transforming the area into a recreational and social center.

At the beginning of the twentieth century a young man known as W.C. Handy had a hit with his recording of *Blues on Beale Street*. This song inspired a generation of blues artists to perform on Beale resulting in the creation of the *Memphis Blues* style. As I'm reading this I can imagine a young Muddy Waters strolling down Beale whistling *Blues on Beale Street*, much in the same way as *Walking in Memphis* drew me here. This must be a lesson to anybody in the process of trying to create a tourist

Mecca; just write a popular song with the name in the title…..now then, what rhymes with Dubai….

I have spent some of my most reflective and pleasurable moments sitting on a terrace; sipping coffee and watching the world go by. My enjoyment is definitely enhanced when I am lucky enough to be in a world tourist destination, such as New York, Paris or Rome. Even as a visitor, sitting in a cafe looking out, I can fantasize about what it would be like to be a local and have the world come to me. Beale Street is such a place, be it on a smaller scale and, with its history and musical heritage, it is unique in the world, attracting an eclectic mix of music lovers. I lost count of how many different languages I heard during the couple of hours of writing postcards.

I wandered around the cosy boutiques looking for souvenirs before heading back to the apartment with a six pack of cold beers for the boys.

My brother and his friends were buzzing from the Stax Museum visit and as we sat on the balcony in the late afternoon sun they filled me in on a bit of the history.

The Stax record label became successful in the 1960's, featuring artists such as Otis Redding, Albert King and Booker T and the MG's, who were actually the house band performing on numerous hits. Due to various problems, the label went into bankruptcy in 1976 and the building deteriorated to such an extent that it was pulled down. Twenty-seven years later the museum opened, built as a replica of the studio and featuring videos, films, photos, instruments and memorabilia from the 'Southern Soul' era. It sounded great but after nearly two weeks together I more than happy with my decision to have a little 'time out'.

The guys went back to their apartment, leaving us to relax and get ready for our big Beale Street debut.

The plan was to meet at B.B. Kings Blues Club later that evening. B.B. King was someone with such a famous name but whom I knew very little about. In fact at that point I knew the name of his guitar but couldn't recall any of his songs. I decided to make an effort and took a few minutes to read up about him, in case the opportunity arose to appear knowledgeable in front of my peers.

Although having always had a passion for guitars, King started life in Memphis as a humble DJ in the 1940's, where he was known as the *Beale Street Blues Boy*. He shortened his nickname to B.B. when he decided to make a career move and become a full time guitarist. He chose to play the hollow-bodied Gibson ES 335, a guitar that became legendary for him and synonymous with *blues* music. King's guitar was famously named after an incident in the 1949 in a bar in Arkansas. Legend has it that two men got into a fight during a gig and managed to knock over a kerosene stove, causing a fire. The building was evacuated but King ran back in, risking his life to save his guitar. When he found out afterwards that the fight had broken out over a girl named *Lucille,* as a reminder never to do anything crazy over a girl, he named all his subsequent guitars after her.

As an early fan of the band *Rush,* I also fell in love with the shape and sound of the guitarist's white ES 335, which inspired me (and many others I'm sure) to learn to play.

Beale Street at night was like another world. A sea of neon blended with a cacophony of music spilling out from every bar, combined with buskers and street acrobats to invade the senses. The crowd had significantly increased as well and we waited patiently in line to enter B.B. Kings. Our friends had already grabbed a table and we studied the menus hoping to find something as tasty as our waitress. We settled for burgers again which might sound a little monotonous but they vary so much from place to place that it's almost like a different meal. These were delicious hickory 'giant' relatives of the burgers we are more familiar with and we savored every mouthful, washing them down with ice-cold beer from the bottle. The band started their show and the night kicked off. We made merry until well into the evening, some of us enticed onto the dance floor to strut our stuff, others content to watch the superb musicians. Highlights of the evening included an amazing guitar solo in a rendition of *Purple Rain* and a medley of soul hits. The band eventually finished their set and we decided to move on.

As possibly the least experienced traveler amongst us, Alex was amazed at the attention he received from several rather pretty ladies. Not wishing to be too harsh on my good friend, time has not been his greatest ally. However, on this particular September evening, his receding hair line and middle-aged paunch seemed to be singularly irresistible to the ladies. At first I think he entertained the thought that either he had been drastically underestimating his sex appeal or maybe that expensive eau-de-cologne was finally paying off. But when, after several minutes of polite conversation, one of the ladies suggested finding a more intimate place, he suddenly cottoned on to what was happening.

To be fair to the women, they took rejection incredibly well and continued walking and talking with us for a while after. During this time we witnessed what was for me the very definition of a charitable act. When one of the prostitutes was confronted by a beggar, without the slightest hesitation she dipped into her handbag and gave him some money. I couldn't help but ask myself if I were in her shoes, would I be as generous or would I be more inclined to hold on to my hard-earned cash. Alex was touched by this scene as well and as we staggered back to our lodgings we both made a resolution to be less judgmental in the years to come.

# *Thirteen*

I awoke to the sound of swishing curtains and the warmth of sun light willing my eyelids to open. I tried to ignore the dull ache behind my eyes and concentrate on the day ahead…. the big day ahead!

We had breakfast in a conveniently situated diner and set off on foot down the clearly signposted route to Sun Studios. One thing that I found remarkable about Memphis is that a couple of hundred meters away from downtown, there seemed to be no leakage of prosperity. The pristine, high-rise buildings were a stark comparison to the seemingly deserted warehouses and garages just around the corner. Here was a part of town ripe for development and, with the agreeable warmth of the southern sun on my back I found myself fantasizing over the possibility of moving here with my family and immersing myself in redevelopment schemes.

I had recently seen a documentary by the news reader Trevor Mc Donald, who had visited Sun Studios on his trip along the Mississippi. Even though I had a good idea of what to expect I couldn't help being blown away by the relative size of this studio, in comparison to its contribution to musical history. If it wasn't for the large sign outside we would have just kept on walking, passing what could be understandably mistaken for just another empty workshop.

We met our friends outside and walked into the tiny reception area to collect our tickets. This room doubled up as a cafe and museum, so as we waited for the next tour, we ordered coffee and perused the many photos and memorabilia. A photo of U2 reminded me that they recorded songs from the brilliant *Rattle and Hum* album at the studio using the rudimentary equipment to maximize authenticity.

After a few minutes we were beckoned into a second, even smaller room and after a brief introduction, were taken up the short flight of stairs to visit the museum section of the building. Our guide showed us around the display cabinets, highlighting the most interesting artifacts, including Elvis's 1955 Martin D28 guitar with custom tooled leather cover. He recounted stories about the early years of the studios creator Sam Phillips. Phillips worked as a DJ and radio engineer for 'Muscle Shoals' radio station in the 1940's. In 1950 he opened the 'Memphis Recording Service', and having a keen interest in 'Blues' music, recorded artists such as B.B.King and

Howlin' Wolf as well as events like weddings and funerals. He launched his own record label in 1952, naming it Sun Records.

We were treated to some early recordings, as well as 'Big Mama' Thornton's song, *Hound Dog*, which reached number one in 1953. This song provoked many copy-cat responses including *Bear Cat* by Rufus Thomas, an almost identical song which later led to a successful copyright lawsuit against Sam Phillips. This in turn necessitated Phillips to sell Elvis Presley's recording contract to RCA.

After a few minutes to walk around the exhibits and take photos, we descended a flight of stairs into the Studio itself. The room can only be described as modest. I would hazard a guess at a quarter of the size of RCA Studio B. Apart from a few instruments dotted around, our attention was drawn to the 1950's microphone stand at the far end, and beside it, a little cross on the floor. This is apparently where Elvis used to stand and sing, with his back to the intimidating face of Sam Phillips behind the recording desk, separated by a glass screen. It's hard to imagine that millions of people have visited this spot to pay homage to Elvis, many kissing the microphone and the cross, including famously Bob Dylan.

As we stood in that room trying imagine the atmosphere sixty years before, our guide told us the legendary story of the day a truck driver from Tupelo knocked on the door.

Elvis visited the studio in 1953 at the tender age of eighteen, to cut a record as a gift to his mother. He played guitar and sang two songs, *My Happiness* and *That's When Your Heartaches Begins* (our guide actually played us the original recording). Sam Phillips was not present that day but his assistant Marion Keisker was obviously taken with Elvis and brought his name up whenever somebody was looking for a singer. He returned to the studio the following January and recorded two more songs, one of which, *Without You*, caught Phillip's attention. Weeks later when he could no longer remember the singer's name, Marion Keisker was quick to remind him of the young truck driver and he agreed to call him up for an audition. Elvis came in and sang every song he knew but was clearly missing a band and so a second session was scheduled with *Scotty Moore* on guitar and *Bill Black* on slap bass to take place at Moore's house. Neither musician was particularly impressed with Presley's singing but they decided to try him one last time in the studio. Sam Phillips recorded several songs but nothing in the style that he was hoping for and so the musicians took a break. Elvis started fooling around at this point and started singing *That's all Right Mama.* When the band joined in, Phillips knew he had found what he was looking for and within hours the song was perfected. The resulting recording received its first airplay that summer and the rest, as they say, is history.

On one of the walls of the studio is a picture of Elvis sitting at the piano with Jerry Lee Lewis, Johnny Cash and Carl Perkins gathered around singing. Apparently Carl Perkins had booked time at Sun to record some new material, bringing the recently discovered Jerry Lee Lewis in to play piano. During the session Elvis Presley, who was now recording with RCA Victor, popped in on a social visit, shortly followed by Johnny Cash. The resulting impromptu jam session was recorded by Phillips and later named the "Million Dollar Quartet" by a local news reporter. Standing there in the actual room, listening to the original recordings of *That's All Right Mama* and some of the quartet sessions was truly spine-tingling.

The Sun Studio tour finished with a photo session, with each of us taking it in turns to pose in front of the 1950's microphone, standing on the cross in a typical Elvis stance.

Next on the agenda was the *Graceland* tour and we headed out into the blistering mid-day heat to await the shuttle bus. The ride to Graceland was pleasantly air-conditioned and during the few miles to our destination, a television showed concert footage of the great man. As we got further out of the town my anticipation mounted, culminating in the closest I can get these days to excitement as we first glimpsed the famous gates and the distant white columns of the front porch obscured by trees.

Expecting to pull into the gardens straight away, I was somewhat perplexed when our bus pulled into a complex of buildings on the other side of the road. As I descended the bus and set my eyes upon rows of Disneyland style gift shops and fast food restaurants I hoped this visit wouldn't be an anticlimax.

We picked up our tickets and chatted with some of the staff who were all polite, knowledgeable and willing to answer all our questions. We had a few minutes to wait and so I took the liberty of connecting to the wifi to fill in some gaps in my knowledge.

Elvis was born in Tupelo, Mississippi on January 8th, 1935, as one of twins and it appears that even his birth was miraculous. In an interview with his father, Vernon Presley in 1978, he recounts the feeling of "utter desolation" at the birth of his still born son *Jesse.* In those days medical science wasn't sufficiently advanced to predict the presence of twins. The young parents had no idea that there was a second baby so when Elvis popped out it was nothing short of miraculous. Although dreadfully poor, the Presley's dreamt of having a large family, trying to fall pregnant again but to no avail and so little Elvis remained an only child, forming a tight bond with his parents. As a young lad he took a trip to the hardware store with his mother Gladys, in the hope of getting a gun. However Gladys had other ideas and, fortunately for the world of music, he came home with a guitar instead. He was introduced to music at a young age, singing gospel in the local church but it was the fortuitous move to Memphis that gave Presley the opportunity to pursue a career in music.

Upon boarding a second shuttle bus we were given an iPad which, being a mild technophobe, immediately struck fear into my heart. However, the staff gave clear, precise instructions and as it turned out was incredibly easy to use; one might even say 'idiot proof'. The bus pulled across the road and the iPad commentary began.

We passed through the wrought iron gates shaped like a book of sheet music, past the stone wall surrounding the grounds built in pink, Alabama fieldstone. I was amazed to see that even now, nearly forty years after his death the wall is covered in fresh graffiti left by well-wishers. Passing up the tarmac drive, the bus stopped right outside the main entrance, the beautiful white portico. This for me would be the culmination of a lifelong, all be it one-sided, relationship with Mr. Presley, and as I exited the bus the sensation was surreal.

We paused for photos outside the front door and we were instructed to turn on our iPads and wander through the house and grounds at our leisure.

Graceland mansion was built in 1939, named after the daughter of the original owner 'Grace Toof'. Presley purchased the house in 1957 for the sum of $100,000 dollars at the age of just twenty-two. In the years that followed he reputedly spent more than half a million dollars on new constructions and renovations, tailoring the estate to his needs.

The first thing I noticed as I walked in was that the stairs and all the upstairs rooms are closed to the public. Apparently the upstairs remains untouched since the day he died and is only visited by close family members. As I stood just inside the front door, I was only meters from the spot where, on that fateful day of 16th August 1977, Elvis Presley collapsed and died of a heart attack in the bathroom directly above.

Wandering through the mansion was not at all the experience I thought it would be. I had imagined being transported through the building at a rate of flow governed solely by the Sistine Chapelesque crowd, my feet occasionally touching the floor in front of the less interesting artifacts. The reality was thankfully completely different. Evidently the group numbers are tightly controlled, with enough time in between each party to minimise any possible bunching.

Although most of the rooms are cordoned off, the scale of Graceland is such that it is possible to get a good view of everything, with plenty of opportunities for photos. First stop was the lounge with its custom made 4.6 meter sofa, backing onto the music room, complete with baby grand piano. On the other side of the entrance hall is the dining room featuring ornate cabinets and a magnificent dining table. I passed his aunt's bedroom and down the few steps to the famous jungle room. Presley created this 'man cave' in the mid-sixties incorporating a waterfall and some pretty wild furniture, reportedly bought to shock his father. In 1976 the jungle room was converted into a recording studio and used during the making of his last two albums. I passed into the modest kitchen, which was still in use up until 1993 by Elvis's Aunt Delta. Downstairs to the basement, I found a billiard room and TV room complete with three TV's, that Elvis would often watch all at once. We were informed that all the rooms were in more or less in the same state as the day he died.

Outside I wandered around Vernon's office, the recreation room, the trophy building and  racquet ball courts; passed the kidney-shaped swimming pool and on to the Meditation Garden. The thing that struck me most was the modesty of the whole thing. This is a man who earned a vast fortune during his lifetime and could have lived in a palatial building anywhere in the world, but instead chose to stay here, surrounded by his family and friends. This speaks volumes about the character of a man that so few people knew but, certainly in his later life, so many people criticised. Something that was not often mentioned in all the bad press he received before and after his death was how incredibly generous he was. His concerts and public appearances often raised huge sums of money for charity and he regularly gave away the most fantastic gifts including cars and houses. Some reports suggest that during his lifetime he earned today's equivalent of a billion dollars and was America's single highest tax payer. So why did he die with only five million to his name? The answer is simple; he gave it all away.

I moved on towards the Meditation Gardens to the Presley's final resting place. Originally buried in the Forest Hill cemetery, Elvis's body was relocated, for reasons of security, to the Meditation Gardens, where he now lies next to his mother, father, and grandmother. I stood by the graves, read the moving inscriptions and, in my own way, paid homage to this polite, humble, good-natured, kind-hearted, vulnerable King of Rock & Roll. One can only feel sadness for what might have been a story with a happier ending. I always remember my mum saying "If he had only come to England, we could have sorted him out". But of course that was never an option as apparently his manager, Colonel Tom Parker, was an illegal immigrant in the US and could never leave for fear of not regaining entry and subsequently never booked any shows for Elvis abroad.

I particularly liked the simplicity of the quote by Grantland Rice on Vernon Presley's grave which, to me, says a lot about the man buried beneath it. It reads:

*"For when the One Great Scorer comes*
*To mark against your name,*
*He writes not that you won or lost,*
*But how you played the game."*

Looking around I could see that my travel companions were experiencing the same quasi- religious experience as I was and we walked in contemplative silence back towards the house.

To end on a high note, we were shown into a large auditorium and treated to some rare film footage of Elvis at his best, before the short shuttle bus trip back across the road.

With our VIP tickets we also had access to the compound containing Elvis's airplanes, the *Lisa Marie* and *Hound Dog II*. The *Lisa Marie* is a vintage Convair 880 airliner, bought by Elvis in 1975 and refurbished to his taste including a lavish conference room, a private penthouse bedroom and bathrooms with gold fixtures. As someone who thinks twice before investing in a new shower head, I couldn't help but reflect on the dazzling luxury that superstardom provides.

I wandered up and down snapping photos, remembering a story. Apparently when Elvis learned that his daughter, Lisa Marie, had never seen real snow, he flew her, along with friends and family, to Denver, Colorado. She happily played in the snow for a few minutes and built a snowman, before hopping back on the plane and flying home to Memphis. I guess that's a good enough reason to have a plane! The *Hound Dog II* is a Lockheed Executive Jet Star, a much smaller, practical plane apparently bought to ferry his manager, Colonel Tom Parker, around.

It became apparent that the Graceland experience was having an effect on us when we paused for refreshments (ordering coffee and cheesy nachos – trust me when I say that these are two flavours that should never be combined! ). The general mood was definitely one of quiet contemplation.

Next on the tour was a building containing some of Elvis's wonderful and wacky collection of vehicles including a Pink Cadillac, Harley Davidson Motorcycles, a Ferrari, a pink Jeep, as well as golf buggies and go-cart contraptions.

The tour would not have been complete without a trip to the numerous souvenir shops to peruse the mostly tacky array of trinkets, similar to those I vaguely recall seeing in shops in the 1970's. Something that did catch my eye was the stunning range of snug-fitting Las Vegas style jumpsuits, available in several colours. We dared each other to try one on, but couldn't quite get past the combination of English reserve and the ever apparent threat of being posted and ridiculed by social media.

Funnily enough, it had fleetingly occurred to me that what Beale Street lacked was an Elvis impersonator and that investing in such a suit might give me the opportunity to launch a new career. But, alas, the dream died in that souvenir shop. Looking on the bright side, the decision probably saved my marriage.

We discussed the tour, all struck by how homely Graceland comes across and how personal the tour is. All the commercial activity has been left on the opposite side of the road, leaving the estate in comparative peace. My brother summed it up nicely with his diary entry:

*"I was struck by how human the experience had been and how one person could make such an impact on this world. I left feeling nostalgic, even homesick for a lost past".*

We passed the bus trip back to downtown in quiet contemplation, testimony that the spirit of Elvis continues to touch people's lives. As for his legacy, like so many artists his persona has made, and continues to make, a huge amount of money. I'm sure it would please him to know that his ability to generate wealth is still contributing to the livelihoods of many.

This would be our last night in Memphis and everybody seemed determined to make the most of it. Nightfall brought welcome respite from the heat, making the stroll into town invigorating.

We met up with my brother's friends at the far end of Beale Street and sat 'al fresco' with oversized beers, chatting to the bar 'barker'. This is the person responsible for encouraging people into the bar using a mixture of charming persuasion and stunning good looks, aimed to penetrate the defenses of the most stubborn passerby.

We headed down a couple of blocks to Huey's, restaurant, tempted by their advertising slogan *Blues, Brews and Burgers.* We were treated to not only a champion amongst burgers, but also two-for-one beer, all in all a good start to the evening. I couldn't resist asking why their ceiling was covered in toothpicks, not indeed a question one asks very often. The waitress disappeared for a minute or two and returned with a bunch of straws and a pack of tooth picks and proceeded to distribute them, giving instruction to fire at will into the polystyrene ceiling tiles. The game, combined with the copious quantities of man-strength beer, was actually highly entertaining, but eventually we ran out of ammo and it was time to move on. We walked the full length of Beale, passing crowds of merry-makers gawking at the street entertainers. Alex was again approached by some rather pretty but dubiously dressed ladies of the night, but any hidden agendas seemed to be bi-passed and nothing was exchanged except pleasantries. We decided to check out Jerry Lee Lewis's bar at the other end of Beale. Lewis opened the *Honky Tonk* in 2013 and has been known on occasion to perform there.

Ever since I first witnessed his unique piano and vocal style, I have always been fascinated by Lewis. The man who played a huge part in the advent of Rock 'n Roll has had many ups and downs in his career, including marrying his thirteen-year-old cousin and subsequently ostracising most of the planet. A notorious hell-raiser, he has defied the old adage 'live fast and die young' by out-living most of his peers. Nicknamed *The Killer*, this religious man was said to be tortured by the sinful nature of his music and was convinced that he and his audience were destined for hell. However there is no denying that the man is a rock and roll genius, described rather aptly as having *one foot in heaven and the other in hell*. Unfortunately for us, that evening there were no impromptu jam sessions by the great man. The bar lady informed us that his next appearance in the *Honky Tonk* would probably around his eightieth birthday, later that month.

On this particular evening the entertainment consisted of a Johnny Cash tribute band. My brother being a huge Cash fan, was in his element and the evening soon progressed from beer to Wild Turkey Whisky. Being a fan of neither Cash nor whiskey, I decided to follow a craving for ice cream and after wishing our friends bon voyage for the following morning, I headed off into the night chaperoned by Alex. My brother told us later that the evening had degenerated as the whisky kicked in. He struck up a conversation with a couple of local guys and when the subject turned to the sensitive issue of racism and white supremacy he decided it was time to leave.

# *Fourteen*

We were due to leave the apartment at nine but when I saw the state of my brother I knew that in order to achieve the deadline, medication was necessary. Eyes like piss holes in the snow, pale as a redhead's lower lumber, he swore that whisky was the spawn of Beelzebub and would never again pass his lips. I was wondering how long it would be before this sentence passed his lips again.

Eventually we managed to get our affairs in order and rejoined our car to try and find a diner for breakfast. Parking in the middle of downtown, I walked a block or two in each direction, searching without luck for a suitable establishment. Eventually, spotting several police cars parked in a row, my brother had a hunch that your average policeman knows the best places to eat. Sure enough they were parked outside a little diner that accommodated us with an exceptional fry-up of eggs over-easy, hash browns, bacon, toast and coffee, served by a lovely waitress (thank you, Memphis Police Department.)

Rejoining our car, we drove a few blocks down to the Civil Rights Museum pulling up outside the Lorraine Motel. Something deep within my brain clicked almost audibly in recognition of the building.

I had recently read the fantastic *Ken Follett* trilogy, mapping the lives of several families through the events of the twentieth century. When I had reached the part set in the sixties I realized that I needed a little more background information to bridge the crevasses in my knowledge of history and so I did a little surfing. During this time I recalled a photo of the assassination of Martin Luther King on the balcony of the building which I now stood in front of. Strangely enough, at no time had it registered in my brain that this event had occurred in Memphis, so for me the surprise at being suddenly confronted by a place of such historic relevance was nothing short of exhilarating.

Something we hadn't bargained for was that on this particular morning the museum was shut. There were however, thanks entirely to this wonderful age of technology, some monitors scattered around on which one can watch short films of the events leading up to the assassination.

On April 3rd, 1968, Martin Luther King was visiting Memphis in support of black sanitation workers, who were striking due to unfair and dangerous working conditions. Unbelievably, city rules cited that the black workers were not allowed to shelter from the rain anywhere but in the back of the compressor trucks with all the rubbish. After the appalling deaths of two black workers, inadvertently crushed to death by a rubbish compressor, the workers walked out.

Having received many death threats, including a threat to blow up his plane to Memphis that day, King added these words to his planned speech, prophesying the events to come:

"Well, I don't know what will happen now. We've got some difficult days ahead. But it doesn't matter with me now. Because I've been to the mountaintop. And I don't mind. Like anybody, I would like to live a long life. Longevity has its place. But I'm not concerned about that now. I just want to do God's will. And He's allowed me to go up to the mountain. And I've looked over. And I've seen the Promised Land. I may not get there with you. But I want you to know tonight, that we, as a people, will get to the Promised Land! I'm so happy tonight. I'm not worried about anything. I'm not fearing any man. My eyes have seen the glory of the coming of the Lord"

Early evening the following day, King left room 306, walked out onto the balcony and was struck by a single bullet to the head, fired from the building opposite. Everything is clearly mapped out, from the trajectory of the bullet to the wreath marking the spot where King fell. Apart from this wreath on the balcony, the exterior of the motel has been left just as it was on the day of the assassination, with King's car still parked out front.

The monitor directly in front of the balcony shows footage and photos leading up to and during the event but there was a small, well dressed old man hogging it, repeatedly pressing the button to watch the sequence over and over again. Having other things to do that day, listed on my highly important tourist's itinerary, after a few patient minutes I asked him if I could watch the short film. He immediately stepped aside in an almost trance-like state and as I moved closer I could see tears in his eyes. I detected the slight odour of alcohol on his breath as he explained to me that he was actually part of a small group of well-wishers, waiting to catch a glimpse of King as he came out onto the balcony on that fateful day. He apparently witnessed the gun shot and the aftermath, memories that in his words "will haunt him forever". He explained that he passed by the Lorraine Motel every day to relive the terrible experience and to pay his respects to the great man.

The cynic in me can think of many reasons to doubt this man's story, but it was hard to deny his genuine strength of emotion and the obvious void the tragedy had left in his life, so many years on.

Unexpectedly touched by the visit, we walked in silence in the blistering heat to our next port of call, the Gibson Guitar factory. We had a guided tour booked for later that morning, but Alex and myself wanted to take the opportunity to arrive early and try out some of the guitars in the shop beforehand. My brother, not sharing our passion for guitars, decided to go and see the *Blues Hall of Fame* and catch up with us for the factory tour after.

There aren't many budding guitarists that don't grow up aspiring to own a Gibson guitar. As mentioned before, I was an early fan of the band *Rush* and instantly smitten with the guitarist Alex Lifeson's white Gibson ES335 but had to content myself with a cheap copy. My friend Alex has worked harder than me and has realized a childhood dream. He is now the proud owner of a small collection of Gibson guitars.

We entered the Gibson building and asked politely if we could try out some guitars. It's funny that after all these years, I still feel as guilty as a schoolboy when asking to try out an instrument that I secretly know that I have no interest in buying. However the guys working in the shop were more than accommodating and, in true

American style, they made us incredibly welcome. We were supplied with guitar picks and were trustily given the run of the shop, which consisted of many thousands of dollars of guitars. There must have been well over a hundred instruments there, ranging from acoustic, semi-acoustic and solid body. All the big names were present, including the SG, Les Paul, ES335 and the iconic Flying V.

A phenomenon of guitar shops that makes it hard for a mediocre player like myself to relax, is that musicians tend to become incredibly competitive during a seemingly innocent guitar trial. The scenario involves two budding guitarists that may, par chance, simultaneously reach up and unhook an instrument from the wall, even on opposite sides of the shop. Maybe it in some way justifies the many hours of finger mutilating practice, but something deems it necessary to protect their artistic pride by exhibiting their best licks and most complex chord sequences. The situation can hastily turn into something reminiscent of the scene from the film *Crossroads*. Alex is very cynical about this. He believes that certain people rehearse a very limited amount of material to a high standard for just such an occasion and exhaust their entire repertoire in so many minutes. I, on the other hand choose to believe that most are genuinely better than me, the brief guitar shop performance being the tip of their musical iceberg. However as luck would have it when we arrived we had the shop to ourselves and so were able to systematically work our way around the walls of guitars playing the obligatory snippets of *Oasis* and *Deep Purple*. After a prolonged visit to the semi-acoustic section we were forced to leave when our egos were threatened by a man in another section playing a couple of well-oiled licks.

We lounged around in the enormous Gibson lobby for a while, being joined by my brother, just as we were handed our plastic safety goggles for the tour.

The factory opened in 1974 and is responsible for the production of all the semi-acoustic or semi-hollow guitars; the solid bodies being made in Nashville and the acoustics in Bozeman, Montana. Hanging in the corridor at the factory entrance are several famous signature guitars including B.B.King's *Lucille* and Scotty Moore's ES 295. After a brief history of the factory, we donned our goggles and entered the workshops. The atmosphere was humid and has to be kept that way in order to the keep the wood from drying out too much. This helps it to remain pliable and prevents cracking during contortion into the various guitar forms. Strolling through the factory, we witnessed all parts of the guitar-making process, from carving out the shape and bending the plywood to attaching the neck and fret board. We stopped at each work station as our guide attempted to explain each process to us, shouting over the noisy machinery. The last stage in the process was the finishing, which involves sanding and painting the guitars. I watched spellbound, in awe of the skill of these artisans as they applied layers of bright lacquer to create the beautiful sunburst finishes. What amazed me is that each guitar is finished by hand, which makes it slightly different in colouration and form and therefore unique; something that justifies to some extent the rather hefty price tag. We managed to leave the building without Alex adding to his guitar collection and walked back into town for our last stop in Memphis.

*     *     *

Being within easy walking distance, there was just enough time to take a look at the five star *Peabody Hotel*. This magnificent building was drawn to my attention by a fellow tourist who took the time to explain to me the details of the famous duck march.

The story starts in the 1930's when the hotel manager, Frank Schutt, returned from a hunting trip and as a prank, he put several decoy ducks in the fountain of the Grand Lobby. Several of the guests were so taken with them that real ducks have been a feature in the hotel ever since. The duck spectacle has become almost legendary over the years and the current day spectacle draws in large crowds.

At eleven o'clock every morning, five ducks are ceremoniously taken from their five star roof top residence, escorted into the lift by the uniformed

Duckmaster and descend to the ground floor lobby. On exiting the lift they follow a red carpet leading to the central fountain and spend the day bobbing up and down in front of adoring guests. At five o'clock the process is reversed and the ducks are led back upstairs by the Duckmaster to their luxury residence (reputedly costing over $200,000, complete with marble floors and ceiling fans – God Bless America!!). I was surprised to learn that several well known celebrities have taken on the honorary roll of Duckmaster, including Steven Fry, Joan Collins, Kevin Bacon, Peter Frampton, Patrick Swayze and Oprah Winfrey.

Entering into the building our eyes feasted on the sumptuous decor of the Grand Lobby, but unfortunately we were too late for the famous ceremony. I became very conscious of the fact that in my flip-flops, shorts and T-shirt I was decidedly underdressed (and sweaty) in comparison to the elegant clientele of the *Peabody*. So contenting ourselves with a brief tour and another fleeting reflection on the stark imparity of life, we returned to our car.

*    *    *

Driving out of Memphis on the Interstate 55, we experienced the kind of melancholy that sometimes occurs after a meaningful achievement. Having had an amazing time in this town, it definitely felt like a chapter in our trip, and maybe in our lives, had closed. The journey proceeded in comparative silence, accompanied only by the sad cadence of Robert Johnson.

Heading south now, we were entering the area of land known as the Mississippi Delta. Stretching for two hundred miles down to Vicksburg and up to seventy miles wide, the land is actually comprised of the delta of the Yazoo River and the Eastern flood plain of the Mississippi river. Famously known as the land of Blues, this genre of music was born out of the toil and hardship of Afro-American slaves. It is said that as early as the Civil War, black soldiers could be heard singing songs in the 'Blues' style, describing the day-to-day hardships using ancient melodies from the motherland.

We decided to stop at Vicksburg situated on the banks of the Mississippi. The town has a rich history going back centuries but is probably best known for its tenacity during the American Civil War. Its situation high on a bluff beside the river made it pretty much impregnable and so the only real tactic available to Union Army was that of siege. The people of Vicksburg bravely hung out for 47 days, eventually surrendering on the point of starvation. The town's eventual submission was considered a major turning point in the war.

We found a cheap motel and asked for non- smoking rooms. Apparently the policy of 'non-smoking' in this particular motel chain must only have been applicable to the room's current occupant, as it was clear that the last people to inhabit the room had asked for a 'smoking' room. After leaving the windows open for a while, our noses became accustomed to the great smell of ash-tray and it was time to go and check out the town.

Leaving the car on the river front, we stumbled upon a very homely bar featuring a terrace, complete with rusty iron table, three chairs and a magnificent view of the river. Settling in with some cold beer in the early evening sunshine, I could feel the despondency of leaving Memphis slipping away already. Ambling on a little further down the river front, we happened upon a bustling sea food restaurant. Although a little over budget my brother kindly offered to treat us to dinner and after some polite (but brief!) protestations we asked for a table. Dinner consisted of deep fried 'gator bites and blackened red fish in a crawfish cream sauce, green beans and salad and was, quite frankly, delicious.

We left with the warm afterglow of having eaten well and decided to take a stroll through the centre of town, which consisted of a mixture of up-market boutiques and old 1970's style shops, including an original coca-cola store. At first the warmly lit shops seemed very homely but as we continued on I realised that we were completely alone. There wasn't even anybody to stop and ask where all the people were. There appeared to be some sort of faint piped music along the street although I couldn't quite work out where it was coming from; the kind of music we are used to hearing before one of the minor characters receives a crossbow bolt in the chest. A little freaked out by the whole thing, we made a hasty retreat back to the safety of our car and headed back to the ashtray for an early night.

# *Fifteen*

After an unexpectedly good night's sleep I awoke refreshed and ready for the next stage of the journey. We went for the early start, heading out on Route 61 with the intention of stopping at Port Gibson for a look around and breakfast.

Named after the first European settler *Samuel Gibson* in 1788, Port Gibson and the surrounding areas were the scene for many furious battles during the Civil War of 1863. Unlike many towns which were burned to the ground, Port Gibson had the good fortune of winning the admiration of General Grant and thus his protection. In true marketing style the local tourist board has come up with the rather catchy slogan "Port Gibson, Too Beautiful to Burn", which I have to agree works rather well.

Driving down the historic, oak-lined Church Street it was evident that many of the historic buildings have survived. Stopping regularly to take photos of the beautifully designed antebellum houses, we came across the Presbyterian Church. This building is quite unique, featuring a large gold hand on the top of its spire with the first finger extended out pointing straight up to Heaven. We snapped away with our cameras making the most of the gold hand contrasting against the blue sky, agreeing that it would definitely pull in more tourists if the sculptor had selected the middle finger to do the pointing.

We headed into the small downtown area with the hope of finding breakfast but there didn't seem to be much in the way of commerce. Instead I read a plaque in remembrance of a bunch of early Blues musicians that went by the name of the *Rabbit Foot Minstrels*. The Minstrels, headquartered in Port Gibson between 1918 and 1950, spent much of their time touring across the South, playing a major role in spreading Blues Music. The "Foots" as they were known, sometimes numbered up to fifty and travelled around in buses and cars carrying a tent in which the performances took place. With a makeshift stage and kerosene lamps they performed not only blues and rock-and-roll but comedy sketches and erotic dancing, all with no amplification using megaphones when necessary.

After a quick food stop in a ubiquitous fast food chain located in the suburbs, we headed south to pick up part of the route known as the *Natchez Trace*. This trail, starting in Nashville and ending in Natchez itself, is apparently the route that the American bison used when migrating between the grazing pastures of central Mississippi and the salt and mineral deposits of the Cumberland Plateau. Native Americans followed the 'trace' of the bison, thus giving the route its name.

Although slower than the interstate highway, it was definitely worth making the detour to Natchez to break the monotony of the Interstate and to see a bit more of the Delta lands.

Perched on a bluff above the Mississippi offering spectacular views, Natchez had a definite opulent air about it. Named after the Natchez Tribe of Native Americans, the first European colonists were the French, arriving around 1716. The City was for a time the capital of the state of Mississippi, attracting wealthy Southern plantation owners arriving in their droves to build luxurious mansions along the river. The town also has a more dubious past, at one time having the second largest slave trade market in the South.

As we drove past mansion after mansion it wasn't hard to believe that during the nineteenth century, up to half the millionaires in the United States lived in and around this area.

As part of my itinerary I expressed an interest to stop at one of the plantations to learn a bit more about the living and working conditions of the plantation slaves. But unfortunately we were due to be in New Orleans that day and did not have the time to do a visit justice. In any case, having already visited Auschwitz, I am well aware of the abject misery humans can inflict upon one another.

We turned east to rejoin the Interstate 55 and crossed the state line into Louisiana, stopping at Amite to refuel the car. Standing at the opposite pump was a local sheriff, a very friendly man but one of the largest (ok, fattest) men I've seen in a while and bear it in mind we had just spent ten days frequenting fast food restaurants in the obesity capital of the world. He chatted to us about the price of fuel and the local area but I'm afraid that what was going through my mind was how this guy could chase anybody further than the end of the donut counter. Then it occurred to me that he probably had enough fire power in his police car to stop a herd of elephants, the only physical excursion needed, being to press the button that opens the car window and take aim.

As we neared our destination I thought back to the last time I had visited New Orleans. As a young man in his prime at the age of twenty-five, I arrived by train from El Paso in much the same state of mind as this time. I had been travelling with a Swedish guy and we had just spent an amazing time over the Mexican border in a town known as Juarez. The place was as seedy as a bird feeder, full of strip joints, and taxi drivers offering their virgin daughters at very reasonable rates. Being used to American prices, we were blown away by the fact that a bucket of ice containing seven bottles of beer was, at that time, around two dollars, about the price of a plate of scrambled egg. The Swedish guy provided all the entertainment as we were followed everywhere by groups of local girls, seemingly mesmerized by his height, blue eyes and incredibly blond hair. I don't know what happened to him after we parted at El Paso station but it wouldn't surprise me at all if he lives in Mexico and has a job in some kind of circus as a cross between a strong man and a freak show. In fact I should have been his manager....damn it.

Anyhow, I got on the train for what seemed like a week, with the intention of stopping at Houston to stay with a girl I'd met at the Calgary Stampede a few weeks earlier. As we crawled across Texas in the days when mobile phones had wheels on them and were too expensive and impractical to travel with, I kept nipping off of the train with a quarter in my hand to try and let this girl know that I was on my way. My calls were to no avail and so when I eventually arrived in Houston and it was raining, in a place that really isn't supposed to rain, I took it as an omen and stayed on the train. I will never know if friendship would have blossomed into romance; if romance would have blossomed into marriage and children; if our first born would have become an astronaut.......Anyway it was obviously not meant to be for reasons that my wife can probably explain better than I can. Needless to say, when I arrived in New Orleans on that day so many years ago I felt very alone, even toying with the possibility of going home. As it was, the sheer vibrance of New Orleans revived me, giving me memories to cherish for a lifetime.

In those days Hurricane Katrina was no more than a draught in someone's attic and I couldn't help but wonder if I would recognize anything after so much time and so much change.

Initially the most striking thing when arriving by car is the vast amounts of water in all directions, in some places as far as the eye can see. Taking the Interstate 10, we passed over the Lake Pontchartrain Causeway which according to record books is the longest continuous bridge passing over water in the world. At a staggering near twenty-four miles long it seemed to go on forever and really is a remarkable construction. How on earth does one go about sinking thousands of concrete supports into an enormous expanse of water, in a perfect line? The conception is truly mind boggling.

Passing houses on stilts with seemingly only boat access, much of the land around the city is at or below sea-level, making the whole area rather a precarious place for a settlement. The City was originally built on slightly higher natural levees along the Mississippi, but as it grew, developers were obliged to expand onto lower lying land. Artificial levees have been constructed since early colonial times, in an attempt to protect the land which is historically prone to flooding from both the river and the sea. Modern day flood protection consists of a series of levees, canals and gigantic pumps which, as we know, failed catastrophically during a hurricane not so long ago. As the pin-prick cluster of high rise buildings magnified I was secretly praying for clement weather during our stay.

We continued into downtown, negotiating the heavy afternoon traffic and headed towards the French quarter. Certain roads and buildings triggered some long forgotten memories, now so distant that I begin to question their authenticity. I remember tramping from the station carrying my heavy backpack and guitar and arriving at a hostel in the middle of a crummy area in the centre of town. Although I couldn't recall its exact location, I know that it was within a short walk of the French Quarter and conveniently had an adjoining bar. By the evening I had made friends enough to party and we walked into the French Quarter for what turned out to be a wild night.

Today we were staying at the plush Hampton Inn and Suites and as we parked our car and approached the building I felt a bit nostalgic for the loss of the adventurous young me.

We were meeting up with Neil, the guy that had originally conceived the idea of a fiftieth birthday road trip during a particularly beery night out with my brother. He was flying in that morning and, as fate would have it, when we arrived at the entrance to the hotel a taxi pulled up beside us and out he popped. As we chatted at reception, it was evident that the transition from the three amigos to the fab four was not going to be entirely painless. By now we had not only slipped into our little three-middle-aged-men habits, but also had had a wealth of experiences that we referred to on a regular basis.

Neil was in the undesirable position of having to join in with a group that has history together. My wife and I are familiar with this feeling every time we go back to Blighty to meet up with groups of old friends. We try and slot back into our old lives for the brief period of the visit but as the years go by, it becomes ever more apparent that we are inadvertently cut out of conversations because of our lack of shared history. After we have discussed children and schools there is always somebody who brings up, with a conspiratorial nod and a wink, that camping trip in Wales, that night at the beer festival in Seend or that pool orgy in Ibiza. It was always "such a laugh" or "you really should have been there".

Anyway, these are the consequences we have to endure for the sometimes rash decisions we make in our lives and this day I think that Neil was regretting not having started at Chicago with us.

Funnily enough, his unease manifested itself with a seemingly uncontrollable urge to find alcohol. The fact that it was only three o'clock in the afternoon, coupled with the still fresh memories of over-indulgence in Memphis, hinted to me that maybe we were not starting the second leg of the trip on the same page. But being the type to never deny a friend, after a brief discussion and the thought of an ice-cold *cheeky beer* as Neil put it, we headed off to the French Quarter to find a bar.

This area is the heart of New Orleans and, as its oldest neighborhood, steeped in history. As long ago as the 1690's the French claimed Louisiana for king and country, naming it after the fabled King Louis XIV. There are French influences everywhere but none more apparent than here in the French Quarter. In the early eighteenth century, Jean-Baptiste Bienville designed the grid layout, naming the streets after French Royal Houses and Catholic saints. In 1763, the City was given to the Spanish after eighty percent was destroyed by fire. The Spanish proceeded to rebuild the area using their own methods, resulting in an architectural style far from synonymous with its name.

Did I mention that Bourbon Street was wild? Unlike the controlled middle-class partying of Broadway in Nashville, or the discernible beer-drinking Blues lovers of Beale Street, the rule book of responsible debauchery can be tossed out of the nearest window to land in a puddle of pissed-soaked puke that signaled 'time to go home' for an earlier customer. It is a veritable Mecca for hedonists everywhere and, as the four of us dipped into the shade between the rows of bars and clubs, with a sense of titillating trepidation I wondered what the *Big Easy* had in store for me this time.

*    *    *

We found a terrace bar and sat listening to a jazz band in the sunshine. At the risk of this scene sounding rather idyllic, I must clarify that I am not the greatest advocate of jazz music. I know the analogy is often made amongst people unappreciative of this particular genre of music that it resembles a load of, without doubt talented musicians, either trying to tune their instruments or all attempting to play different songs at the same time. As someone who considers himself open to an eclectic musical range I feel quite ashamed to admit that I can recognize an element of truth in this.

Trying to ignore the music, I turned my attention instead to watching a rather incontinent pigeon repeatedly evacuating its bowels on a statue. During the two beers that we consumed there it miraculously pooped his body weight over an unassuming bronze of some evidently unlucky jazz musician. My mind wandered back home to a fridge magnet in our kitchen with the wise old adage "some days you're the pigeon, some days you're the statue".

At the risk of the day's festivities peaking too early, we decided to stretch our legs in the direction of the river front to check out the possibility of a river cruise the following day. I pressed for a trip I had taken on my last visit, up the river to a battle field and back, secretly hoping to trigger some distant memories buried somewhere deep in my addled brain.

After booking our trip, our attentions turned to a rather good band performing in a bar on the keyside. Playing a mélange of Blues and Country, it was enough to entice us in for a something to eat. We watched in awe as the fiddle player sped up and down his tiny violin neck. I have often dreamt of learning to play the violin but where does one start? It's hard enough playing the guitar with its accommodating frets to show exactly where the notes are but there is no such luxury for fiddle players. Not only do you have to guess where the notes are, sometimes at speeds far superior than your average neuron can transmit a signal, but all you get to make the sound is a horse's tail tied to a stick. Add to that a little lubrication in the form of half a bottle of Irish Whisky and a rowdy crowd of bearded revelers spilling beer all over the floor and you have your average fiddlers working conditions. If I had been sporting a hat on this particular afternoon I would have undoubtedly removed it as a solitary act of respect to all you fretless wonders.

Another round of beers later and the accommodating waitress brought us a steaming pot of Gumbo. I was, as far as I can remember, a Gumbo virgin but always keen to try a local dish, especially when it smells as inviting as this did.

This viscous stew appeared to originate in Southern Louisiana during the eighteenth century. It is usually made using meat or shellfish combined with stock, cayenne peppers, celery and seasoning. More commonly served with rice, it was presented to us in a cup with French style bread and was, quite frankly, delicious.

We made the short walk back to the hotel and freshened up before joining Neil in a plush bar opposite our hotel. It was one of these designer affairs with hundreds of bottles of overpriced liquor sitting on glass shelves, with a backdrop of subtly lit mirrors. If I had to sum up the clientele in one word, it would undoubtedly be 'smug'. From their crisp pressed suits, embossed neck ties, flash Swiss time pieces (why don't they just call it a watch) and sun tans, it is a look that no doubt their tailor says oozes successful, sophisticated professional, but to me screams arrogant, deluded dick-head.

Now one thing myself and Neil don't seem to have in common is a love of the above mentioned bars. This is probably down to two basic differences. He is used to being well dressed and fits in nicely with the executive clientele. I, on the other hand, spend my normal days dressed like Worzel Gummidge, blending in nicely with the rest of rural France. For some reason I have always felt uncomfortable in any kind of designer clothing or anything sporting a miniature iron on the label. The long and short of it is that I don't possess any smart clothes and as a result, do not want to drink in anything that resembles the bar we were in. My second objection is, erring in the direction of parsimonious, for me a drink at a bar is only worth so much. I would much rather stay at home than have to suffer the anxiety of having unknowingly spent a proportion of my children's education on a couple of glasses of pissy liquid. OK, I agree that there was a little value added by the pretty barmaid with the skin tight micro-skirt working on this specific evening, but sitting there watching her duplicitous flirting and false familiarity in the hope of a Wall Street Christmas bonus-sized tip was quite frankly embarrassing. OMG, am I becoming a sanctimonious hypocrite. The truth is that of course the attention of a pretty girl massaging an old man's ego is worth a few bucks.

For some, I'm sure that paying several dollars for what the Australians would call a *stubby* and downing in it one gulp in some way justifies passing through life in a well paid but unfulfilling job. On the other hand, maybe I'm just jealous because I can't afford the lifestyle!

As the alcohol began to take effect the barmaid was becoming even more attractive but the thought of the bill was dampening my ardour. It was time to move on, so without further ado we kicked back our chrome plated leather upholstered bar stools and walked out over the shiny marble floor to exit the building.

We headed back to Bourbon Street which was by now heaving with punters as night fell and the bars lit up. As we strolled down the centre of the road we were quickly enticed by the persuasive banter of the entrepreneurial bar staff, into a large bar, in which a superb band were performing.

Bands here seem to cater for every eventuality and this was no exception. The lineup included a number of vocalists and musicians capable of performing everything from Rock and Blues to Soul and Jazz Funk, all to a breathtaking standard. More beers followed and we settled in for a while.

It was around this time that I noticed Neil getting chatty with a pretty young girl wearing not the most practical attire. She had a massive belt strapped around her waist with a pouch at the front resembling something like a human kangaroo. The pouch was stuffed with copious quantities of test tubes and syringes in varying colours. Having made a middle-aged pact not to drink anything unless we could more or less identify the contents, I was surprise to see Neil neck a couple of tubes like a student on fresher's week. He then proceeded to bring out a wad of dollars, peeling off what must have been a very approximate calculation, doubtlessly weighted heavily in the girl's favour. He generously bought us a round and I sipped the coloured liquid, suspiciously thinking that it might blow the back of my head off. It was actually surprisingly weak and tasted of sugar.

While we stood and appreciated the band, even daring to venture onto the dance floor for a great rendition of *Soul Man*, I could see that Neil was talking intently with the 'shot' girl, stopping only to refuel on the rainbow-coloured liquid. Her progressive sales technique became more intimate as she held the round end of the tube in her mouth and expertly decanted its contents into Neil's awaiting orifice, provoking whooping from passersby. Forcibly encouraged by the enthusiastic crowd, she brought out the syringes of vodka jelly, at which point we decided to vacate. By then our friend was over the edge and steadfastly refused to leave the bar and so we wished him luck and moved back out onto the crowded street.

We stumbled upon a miniscule pizza restaurant a little further along, which my brother described as dodgy but I was convinced it had to be good judging by the sole fact that it was full of locals. We sat on stools and ate huge triangles of deep-pan covered in piping hot cheese and pepperoni whilst chatting to the friendly clientele. Feeling refreshed and with stomachs lined it was time to check out some more bands.

Night had firmly fallen now and the many balconies overlooking the Street were teaming with people in various states of dress and undress. Tourists and locals alike wandered in mass in and out of bars carrying their drinks with them, this area being one of the few in the United States to allow street drinking. We passed bars with some great names like Fat Tuesday and Cat's Meow, and there is even a Rodeo Bar complete with mechanical bull. I won't even try to imagine the puddles of puke under that the next morning.

We ended up in one of the larger bars whose name has slipped my mind, probably due to the fact that we were getting fairly 'well oiled' at this point. The band playing was very much of the *Earth Wind and Fire* ilk, even down to the smolderingly tight brass section. As I stood there mesmerized by the predominantly African-American musicians something occurred to me. I definitely have a thing for black bass players. There is something in their charisma and flamboyant style that I find riveting. I find my eye being drawn away from even the prettiest singer or most talented guitarist, to stare rather unnaturally at a middle-aged  overweight man, often sporting dreadlocks and some kind of 1970's cape. They always play the obligatory hyper cool five-string bass with ease and precision, instinctively marking the beat with an exaggerated head nod, every now and then breaking into *slap style* just to emphasise their mastery of the instrument.

As the band played a medley of funky seventies disco hits, my brother and I had no option other than to strut our stuff. I have been relentlessly teased by my offspring for my somewhat unimaginative dance style, but in my defence, when I was their age, popular dances, if they can be called that, consisted of the Pogo, head-banging or a kind of Ska shuffle. It never really seemed necessary to practice individual dance moves for hours in front of a mirror. It was always just a case of drink some alcohol and see what happened. Anyway in this bar the music turned out to be so eclectic that I'm sure that any prior dance knowledge would have been a handicap.

We had a great time well into the night, with Alex looming in the shadows taking photos and my brother and I dancing and singing along with the band. Finally we were full of beer and it was time to crawl back to the hotel, unavoidably purchasing a bag of mini- burgers en route.

We arrived back in our rooms relieved to find Neil stumbling around alive and well, having seemingly returned quite a bit earlier. The lovely lady had remained good friends with him right up until his last dollar, at which point she unaccountably transferred her affections to somebody else.

With the air thick with expletives interspersed with 'bitch' and 'dollars', I decided to retire for the night.

As I lay there drifting off into slumber, I flashed back to my previous visit to the City. I remembered wandering back to the hostel in the twilight hours of the morning after a big night out. Along the upswept pavements I passed wallets, emptied and discarded, syringes and used condoms. Twenty five years on and this New Orleans seemed safer and cleaner, a thought that I found very reassuring.

# *Sixteen*

For the umpteenth time in a row I woke up feeling like I had an embryonic child floating in the cavity behind my eyes pounding to be released. However, on this particular morning, I was a picture of health compared with my shot-gulping friend. Looking a little sheepish he confessed to not remembering anything of the last three hours of the previous evening. What he did know after a quick glance in his wallet was that the adventure had set him back a cool three hundred dollars. Despite the cerebral pain after several cups of coffee we all felt a little more positive and were ready to start the day.

Leaving Neil to do a little work in the hotel room, we headed down through the French Quarter, taking photos of the beautiful buildings with ornate balconies, often enshrouded with kaleidoscopic flower boxes and potted greenery. Apart from the street cleaners we virtually had the place to ourselves and in the glow of the morning sun it bared no resemblance to the hedonistic paradise we visited only hours before. I searched in vain for something that looked familiar from my previous visit, in particular a restaurant balcony which had been the scene of a first embrace. I can honestly say that twenty-five years on I recognized absolutely nothing, which I found rather bemusing given that I can vividly recall wetting myself in preschool almost half a century ago.

I did remember visiting a little flea market at the opposite end of the French Quarter and as it was clearly marked on our map we decided to take a look in search of souvenirs.

Pretty soon the combination of what was becoming a very warm day, coupled with dehydration from our exertions the previous night, lead us in search of water and a little respite from the heat. Locating the street market we crossed the road and entered the old United States Mint, which has a ground floor museum, free admission, great air-conditioning and a water fountain. What a find! The people working on reception were lovely and although the subject matter was of very limited interest we managed to meander through the exhibits for a good half an hour. We received a text from Neil to say that he was waiting for us at the market and so we crossed the road to join him.

Now I may well have imagined this but I would have swore on the life of one of my turkeys that the last time I passed through here the people in the French market spoke French. Back then the only French I knew came from the Beatles, Abba and Labelle – I'll let you work it out. Now after fifteen years in France, I was looking for an opportunity to impress with what I consider a reasonable accent and a vastly improved vocabulary. It was not to be. Either I dreamed that it was French or the hurricane washed it all away. In any case the French flea market of today is about as French as the policeman in 'Allo Allo'. That's not to say that it wasn't interesting. The vendors sold all number of things from T shirts and jewelry to local artwork, herbs, spices and antiques. Desperately trying to find a souvenir that wouldn't be greeted with disdain by my teenage boys, I stumbled across a market stall selling amputated alligator heads. They came in various sizes and were sealed with lacquer, presumably to stop them from rotting. The deal was done and with my brother willing to invest in some as well we managed to beat the hard-nosed vendor down to a reasonable price. Swerving through the rest of the market I stopped only to buy some Gumbo mix which I'm afraid to say is still sitting unused in the cupboard six months on.

Walking back via the magnificent St Louis Cathedral, we dropped our gifts off at the hotel and proceeded back to the river front for a pot of gumbo before the boat trip.

One of the most memorable experiences from my previous trip was the Mississippi Riverboat cruise and I was really looking forward to doing it again. As we boarded our vessel the 'Creole Queen', I was not entirely convinced that it wasn't the same boat as before. The cruise however would be very different. All those years ago I met a girl during my trip down the river. The meeting turned into romance which lasted several happy months which for me in those days was a lifetime.

The Creole Queen is a splendid replica of a paddle steamer complete with huge turning paddle at the back, only emitting diesel fumes in the place of steam. I'm pretty sure that if we lifted the old beast out of the water we would spot some cheeky propellers underneath as well, but these minor technicalities were not going to spoil my day.

The itinerary consisted of a cruise a few miles up the river to the site of the deciding battle between the British and American forces in 1815. There, on the original battlefield, a park ranger was to give us a narrative of the battle. Our riverboat guide introduced himself and without further ado we cast off.

Passing a variety of industries our guide pointed out a large cargo vessel in the process of being loaded with sugar. He explained that over the centuries much of the area's wealth has been generated by the so called *white gold*. In a surprisingly brief amount of time the banks of the Mississippi turned green as we continued through countryside. As the boat followed the meander of the river, I found myself constantly relocating into the shade to escape the blistering heat whilst our knowledgeable guide filled us in on some of New Orleans complex local history.

The area was first settled by the French in 1718, naming it New Orleans in honour of the Duke of Orleans. After the British defeated the French in India, the 1763 Treaty of Paris ceded Louisiana to the Spanish to avoid it falling into British hands. The Spanish held the region for the next forty years during which a massive influx of American settlers made governing problematic. So in 1800 the Spanish, keen to rid themselves of the troublesome area, signed a secret agreement with Napoleon returning Louisiana to the French in exchange for six battle ships and a smidgeon of Italy. Aware of the agreement and realizing the strategic importance of the area, President Jefferson attempted, without success, to buy some of the land around New Orleans with the intension of creating an American port. However, Napoleon was in a vulnerable position. He was on the brink of war with the British and didn't have the resources to protect Louisiana. The Brits', on the other hand, had a large naval presence in the Caribbean, within striking distance of the city. Napoleon was fixated with keeping the area from enemy hands at any cost, writing "The English shall not have the Mississippi which they covet". Running out of options he instructed the sale of the whole of Louisiana to the Americans for $22,500,000, or the equivalent of sixty-four cents an acre or, to put it another way, the deal of the century. The acquisition was the size of The British Isles, France, Germany, Spain, Belgium and the Netherlands combined and it doubled the size of the nineteenth century United States of America.

We continued up the river passing ships that may well have followed the same journey as us from the great lakes. Eventually mooring at the historic battlefield of Chalmette, the boat emptied and everybody filed towards a huge oak tree and our awaiting park ranger. He greeted us warmly and started to recount the battle of 1815.

During the months around Christmas in 1814, the British marched on New Orleans under General Pakenham with the intention of taking control of the city and subsequently regaining control of Louisiana. The Americans, led by General Jackson and having been forewarned, had had time to create various lines of defence. After brief periods of conflict and a catalogue of errors by the British, including forgetting to bring the ladders necessary to cross the canals and digging a shoddy waterway to give their boats access to the area which promptly collapsed, they finally arrived at Chalmette.

The Americans were outnumbered two to one but luck was on their side. The morning of the battle the British crossed the canal onto the battlefield disoriented by thick fog. At the worst possible moment the fog lifted giving the

Americans the perfect opportunity to gun them down. The defeat was nothing short of embarrassing - just 240 American casualties compared to a staggering 2,286 for the British (although rumour has it that after the battle another 500 British soldiers stood up and surrendered after playing dead on the battle field!)

As we stood in the shade of that beautiful oak, listening to the tale of misery and death, it was unavoidable not to become reflective.

It's hard not to be incredibly thankful that we are on this planet at this precise moment in time and live in countries currently at peace. We could have been born in the lawless dark ages, during the period when bubonic plaque ravaged the world or during the World Wars having to suffer untold misery in the trenches or even now in one of the many countries continually ravaged by starvation, disease and war. Ok, who knows what the future has in store for us, but at least we are in the incredibly fortunate position to say that, even if it all ends tomorrow, we have lived in this moment. A moment that I believe will be remembered as the pinnacle of humanity. Speaking for myself and those around me we have enough food, we have medical science on our side, we have peace, we have the capability to earn a decent living and to spend it on things that enhance our lives, and we live in civilizations which are, for the most part, safe and caring. The problems of the future; pollution, climate change, political unrest... have not reached us yet and to quote somebody famous we really have "never had it so good". We will never be able to thank those countless lost generations that nurtured our respective gene pools through starvation and freezing cold, through the lawless, disease ridden eras of history, giving us the opportunity to enjoy our day in the sunshine.

When the park ranger had said his piece, we all wandered up to the visitors centre to look at battle plans and uniforms and to invest in some ice-cold bottled water. We strolled back across the park stopping only to pose artily for photos, attempting to mimic a famous album cover of the eighties and failing miserably, before rejoining our boat. Funnily enough the return trip was pretty similar but animated by our guide in an extremely interesting and heartfelt narrative of the events during Hurricane Katrina. Although we had all seen the news coverage and heard the statistics, listening to somebody that had actually lived through it was quite an emotional experience.

In late August 2005, a hurricane building up in the Gulf of Mexico grew to category five and was named Katrina. On the 28th August, temporary levees were constructed with sandbags and the city was ordered to evacuate, causing traffic jams that our guide described as Biblical. Downgraded to category three, but still immensely powerful, the storm hit southeast Louisiana on the 29th August with devastating consequences. Winds deflected by tall buildings reached recorded speeds of 175 miles per hour, picking up debris (cars, houses, boats) and smashing it against all in its way. The failure of more than fifty drainage canals and levees are now considered to be amongst the worst engineering disasters in history.

By August 31st, eighty percent of New Orleans was under water, in parts as deep as 4.6 meters. Only the French quarter and the Garden district were spared. Although most of the population had been evacuated, those with no access to vehicles or news coverage stayed in the city and were housed in the Louisiana Superdome. As the stadium became overcrowded people turned to the Convention Centre which managed to escape the flooding being slightly above sea level. During the days that followed there were wide spread reports of rape, robbery, drug use and murder in the overcrowded buildings. Bodies were left to decompose where they lay and there was no supply of fresh water or food in the blistering summer heat.

When the storm dissipated it was estimated that up to two thousand people had lost their lives, over 200,000 homes were damaged or destroyed and more than 800,000 citizens had been displaced. The estimated repair bill was in the region of $108 billion.

As our guide wrapped up the story, his voice was thick with emotion and bitterness at the lack of financial support given by the United States government in the aftermath of the storm. All we could do was to thank him for his heartfelt account and head back to *terra firma* and the luxurious respite of our air conditioned hotel room.

\*         \*         \*

After the previous night of excess we decided to avoid the temptations of Bourbon Street and head instead in the direction of the Louis Armstrong Park.

Crossing the road into the French Quarter we meandered up the empty Royal Street admiring the beautiful Creole townhouses. Here's something else I didn't know - 'Creole' is the name given to the descendents of the original European settlers, in this case mostly Spanish and French. Although the word has evolved over the centuries it is thought to originate from the Spanish verb *criar* meaning "to raise". There are many Creole colonies all over the world but for me the word is synonymous with this great city.

We turned down St Ann Street passing yet more brightly coloured buildings, some stylishly rounded off, softening their architectural edges presumably to facilitate the limited turning circle of ancient carts.

One thing you notice about the French Quarter is that Bourbon Street seems to acts like a decoy, attracting all the rowdy unwanted tourists, keeping them amused whilst the other streets exist in a state of blissful tranquility.

Crossing the road we entered into the park dedicated to the great jazzman Louis Armstrong and were greeted by a wall of music coming from somewhere within. On the warm September night the atmosphere was buzzing. Food venders lined the pathways exhibiting enormous pots of bubbling gumbo and Cajun jambalaya. Wrestling with the temptation to eat straight away, we moved quickly on instead to the source of the music; a large stage set up in the centre of the park. The band played their own Cajun version of jazz funk, a sound that evidently went down well with the audience. As I studied the crowd, everybody was dancing with a veritable *joie de vivre* from the youngest child to the oldest grandmother. Their movements were so fluid and natural that I can only presume that the ability is passed on genetically. These people were manifestly not tourists, they were local families enjoying their city.

My brother and Alex joined the long queue for a beer whilst I slipped away for a quick tour of the park. There wasn't a great deal to see but the sculptured ponds were delightful and the bronze statue of Mr. Armstrong was remarkably pigeon free. Louis Armstrong was born in New Orleans in 1901 and like Elvis, his is a true 'rags to riches' story, culminating in international success with songs such as *The Vie en Rose* and *What a Wonderful World*.

From my vantage point on the bridge, I looked back on the undulating crowd enjoying the evening's entertainment and got inkling as to why people stay in a place so prone to flooding and natural disaster. They occupy an area of the world that is steeped in history, *their* history. For centuries their ancestors have fought both each other and the elements, investing their lives and deaths, to live here. To abandon this great city would be to forsake their heritage.

Deterred by the long queues for beer, we headed off into the French Quarter in search of food. We ended up at 801 Royal, one of the restaurants recommended by our cruise guide for serving supposedly one of the best *po'boy* sandwiches. A *po'boy* is a traditional Louisiana sandwich consisting of usually beef, chicken and seafood wrapped up in crisp New Orleans style French baguette. I ordered the classic shrimp version which was overflowing with the deep fried crustaceans, presented with fries and a side salad. Heaven on a plate!!

Heading through the back streets, we passed many of what I would describe as luxurious restaurants; beautifully lit, crisp white table cloths and immaculately presented staff. I made a mental note to bring my family here to eat in such a restaurant when I win the lottery;

closely followed by another mental note to start playing the lottery.

Ending up in a bar known as *The Old Absinthe House,* we unexpectedly stumbled upon an old jukebox. When I first started drinking in pubs, one of the highlights of the evening was to trawl through the song menu of the jukebox and then wait for what always appeared to be an eternity until one of my selected songs came on. What made it so special was the fact that I usually had to endure several hours of shite music beforehand, which in hindsight had the effect of making my song choices all the sweeter. Those were the days when music still had the capacity to shock. I loved to watch the expressions on the older generations' faces when their usual blend of Bonny Tyler and Tina Charles  was blown out of the water by the latest Jam single or a of hard hitting Clash number. Rather sadly, I found it empowering to stick on a few B-sides, waiting impatiently for a curious friend to remark 'I don't recognize this one', allowing me to nonchalantly step in and bamboozle my peers with my profound musical knowledge. I know, I know, I'm a sad act or as my American comrades might put it "whatever". I can't help but feel in this age of technology where everything is on demand all the time, the simple thrill of anticipation has been somewhat lost.

Luckily for us it seemed as if nobody had even noticed this splendid machine, so we chose at will, amusing ourselves trying to get a reaction from the locals. Sadly nothing worked, not even so much as an approving nod in our direction and so it was time to move on.

Avoiding the vast crowds of merrymakers we headed up to the far end of Bourbon Street. The sound of ivories being masterfully tinkled stopped us in our tracks as we approached an inviting looking bar and terrace. We had inadvertently stumbled upon Laffite Blacksmiths Shop which is reputed to be the oldest structure in the USA continuously operating as a bar. Jean Laffite constructed the blacksmiths in around 1720, at which time it served not only horses but also as a headquarters to an infamous pirate gang. The building was used as a hideout and meeting place where the pirates would plan the next dastardly deed and sell contraband goods. The Laffite brothers were captured in 1814 but went on to help General Jackson kick British butt in exchange for a legal pardon. Apparently no one can substantiate this story but it undeniably adds charm to what is already a delightful drinking hole.

The interior of the bar was banged out with enthusiastic revelers singing along with the piano music, so blessed with another glorious evening we decided to take our refreshments on the terrace.

The first time I was here there was quite a big deal made about a famous New Orleans cocktail known as the Hurricane. A delicious blend of rum, fruit juice and grenadine, the creation is credited to local bar owner Pat O'Brien. The experience then was to buy a large cup of the stuff and wander about all night refilling it from the numerous venders up and down Bourbon Street. This time the respective venders seemed to have disappeared, so when the barman at Laffite proposed to make us a Hurricane we enthusiastically agreed. Watching open mouthed as he filled the seven ounce highball glass half full of rum, I started making a mental appointment with the doctors to get my poor liver checked out upon my return.

After a second Hurricane, a large group from inside moved on to another bar, so we shuffled in and found some bar stools next to the piano. The pianist was not only a talented musician but also a superb singer, seemingly able to turn his hand to anything. With the aid of an iPad he could find the chords and lyrics to any song, charging five dollars for each request. The guy had a constant stream of dollars flowing into his tip-pot and I calculated that he sang about twenty songs an hour, five hours a night, that's five hundred bucks thank you very much. Ok, I suppose if you factor in the thousands of hours it takes to become proficient on an instrument it may seem a little less lucrative, but if one can manage to steer clear of laryngitis and the IRS there are worse ways of making a living.

We sang our hearts out to renditions by the Commodores, Queen and Billy Joel, culminating in a particularly raucous rendition of Swing Low, a gift from the pianist in honour of the recent rugby World Cup. We left effectively unable to talk, practically unable to walk, with the warmth of rum in our bellies and joy in our hearts. We made it back to the hotel in what was to be our last night in New Orleans feeling as if the trip had peaked. The big question on our lips - how could we keep this up for another week?

# Seventeen

We all awoke jaded from our recent exertions and today, after travelling through what seemed like a succession of big cities, I for one was ready to head for the sunny beaches of Florida.

This was to be the first time during the trip that we would experience four in the car and although there was ample room, I was intrigued to see if there would be any potential characters clashed.

Pulling out of the city, heading east on the Interstate 10 it was immediately apparent that things had changed. Up until now I had accepted my brothers rather low key road trip playlist, not because it was my music of choice, but more to avoid confrontation (of which I seem to attract rather a lot). Also he played it at such a low volume that it barely had any impact on our immediate ambience. Given the choice, I much prefer to listen to local radio. I love the lottery aspect of radio listening and let's face it, if I don't like the song I just flick around the stations. This has the added bonus of being able to listen in on snippets of local news and the often intriguing 'phone in' conversations. In my local region of France, I regularly eavesdrop on candid afternoon debates with subjects ranging from sex toys and the female orgasm, to "my husband is having an affair, how can I prolong it so the useless bastard leaves me alone". The vast eclectic selection of America radio stations, coupled with amusing 'phone in' subjects to the tune of 'my five year old daughter possesses the power to heal animals' or 'my cousin wants to marry his neighbours horse', to me defines entertainment.

Anyway today, with Neil riding shotgun, the day started a little differently. His first task was to unplug my brother's mp3 player and put it in the glove box. Plugging in his own machine he explained that he had made his own road trip play list, consisting of over three thousand songs (ok, I am exaggerating a little for effect) and he proceeded to turn the volume up to a number we hadn't previously known existed. The first song may have been the Black Crows or something of that ilk and I watched my brother visibly wince in the driving seat as the opening guitar riff ripped into his ear drums. Fortunately it wasn't so loud in the back and I actually quite enjoyed the selection of rock songs that ensued.

I was astonished by his musical knowledge. Not only could he recall the histories of apparently all the bands on his play list, but also those of individual members, focusing on deaths, suicides and incestuous bloodlines right back to Robert Johnson. Yes, Neil had arrived in earnest and we were going to get along just fine.

When we reached the state line and crossed into Alabama, it was time for some Lynard Skynard played at a respectful volume. Although our time in the state was destined to be brief (Alabama is only about 85km wide at this point) I expressed a wish to stop and hear the local accent to see if I could detect any difference in comparison with the Louisianan accent. Passing what initially looked like an old army dump with tanks and planes scattered about on a stretch of grass, we did a U-turn to take a closer look. On closer inspection, we had inadvertently happened upon the Battleship Memorial Park. Intrigued, we parked in the car park and exited our air conditioned environment into a wave of heat, resembling that of opening the oven door to check on the Sunday roast. Unperturbed we grabbed our cameras and set off.

Dominating the skyline was the colossal battleship, the USS Alabama, with a Second World War submarine moored alongside. In the field next to it was a B52 bomber with several fighter planes, tanks, rockets, helicopters and guns. As we meandered around snapping photos it occurred to me that a number of the plane cockpits were cracked and damaged. Now I don't confess to know much about planes, but I'm guessing that the material used to make these covers must be able to withstand at least your average seagull smashing against it at a thousand miles per hour.

A shirtless man happened to be crossing the car park at the same time as us, with the assured gait of an ex-soldier at ease with his surroundings, so I decided to fire a question at him. The guy was in superb physical shape but, as I got nearer, I could tell by his well-leathered skin that he must have been well into his sixties. I asked him about the cockpits and he explained in his smooth Alabaman drawl that the damage was done by hurricane Katrina, more than ten years ago. Apparently many of the exhibits were destroyed beyond repair and the gift shop and workshops were submerged for days. Our new friend showed us around his workshop where he was in the process of re-spraying Ronald Reagan's old helicopter, which was to become the latest addition to the museum. It appeared that he had single-handedly renovated all these planes and he was understandably proud of the fact. When I jokingly asked him what he did in his spare time, he explained that he also took part in Strongman competitions, which amongst other things involved swimming in open sea water. The conversation moved on to sharks, which for me tend to be inextricably linked with sea bathing thanks to the genius of a certain Mr. Spielberg. He explained that he wears an old nineteen sixties type, bright yellow swimsuit, which he assured me scares the sharks off! I couldn't help but reflect on the fact that this guy seemed to do more during his so-called retirement than the majority of people do in a lifetime. As we thanked him for our spontaneous tour and walked back to the car, I must admit that I felt a little inadequate.

By this stage hunger was setting in and, as luck would have it, just up the road was Felix's Fish Camp Grill. From the outside it resembled a stack of driftwood but the interior turned out to be charming. Decorated with an array of flotsam and jetsam and some stunning old photographs, the place was oozing character. It was virtually impossible to choose between all the delicious things on the menu, so on the recommendation of our friendly waitress I went for their best seller; the crab soup. It arrived in no time and consisted of ample amounts of juicy crab meat seasoned to perfection. It really was the very definition of a culinary delight. When we went to pay the bill, the waitress even gave us take away cups of a beverage of our choice at no extra charge. I hesitated to make a suggestion that she should start a hospitality training school in Europe but it seemed like she was doing just fine here.

On exiting the building, Neil and I took a quick peek around the back to catch a glimpse of the stunning sea views, inadvertently happening upon a row of pelicans. Lined up like soldiers, each standing on a weather-beaten wooden post, it presented him with the perfect photo opportunity to remind us forever of our very brief but enjoyable visit to Alabama.

Crossing over the Florida border, we entered into an area known as the 'panhandle'. I'd actually never heard of this region but on closer inspection of our road map I suppose if you take the basic shape of the state of Florida, half-close your eyes and swallow a couple of tabs of LSD, I image it could resemble anything you like.

We pushed on to Tallahassee and stopped for coffee at a junk food restaurant with free wifi, hoping to book some accommodation on the Perdido Key. Everything appeared to be full but we left the Interstate and decided to head in that direction anyway.

When Neil had suggested Perdido as our first destination in Florida, I hadn't equated the name with anything recognizable. However closer scrutiny revealed that it was in fact home to the famous Flora-Bama beach bar, the subject of a video clip I had recently seen on a country music programme. I'm sure the film was cleverly edited but, for some obscure reason, the blend of white sand, boats moored within beer distance of the beach, live music and bikini clad beauties flashing their breasts to all and sundry came across as rather appealing.

Arriving in Perdido, we checked the tourist centre and they duly confirmed that all but the most expensive hotels were full. We drove down the Perdido Key to at least set eyes on the famous bar.

It is named 'Flora-Bama' as it sits right on the Florida – Alabama state line. The original bar, dating back to the nineteen sixties, was built on the state line as a clever ploy to outflank the law. Due to stringent alcohol regulations in Alabama, liquor was cheaper and more available in neighboring Florida. The bar built up a healthy clientele in both states until it was flattened by a hurricane a few years later. It operated out of tents, trailers and cabins for a number of years during the lengthy reconstruction. The bar was re-born using the salvaged original materials and is now apparently a Mecca for party-animals, although we could not substantiate this as we had to move on.

Driving down the coast we stopped at the tourist centre in Pensacola to inquire after accommodation in the area. I was astounded by the amount of supersized, heavily tattooed people milling around. The nice lady explained to us that due to a food festival on the beach (ah-ha!), there were no rooms available in the immediate area; however she did manage to find us a place in neighboring Navarre.

Cruising down the beach boulevard, we pointed out all the places we might have stayed if Lady Luck had been on our side, or if we had had the foresight to book early. I think it was agreed there and then that it's ok to be spontaneous as long as one is willing to pay the price of compromise.

Following the beach road, we made for Navarre and found our motel. We checked in and after what seemed like a lifetime in the car, made for the beach for a first dip in the sea. The water was warm and full of little unidentifiable beasties that thankfully scattered under threat from my hulking great feet. Deciding to test the swimming pool, we were eaten alive by some sand flies that, judging by their voracious appetites, were rather partial to our sweet European blood. Fortunately I know from experience that several years on, when thumbing through the holiday snaps, the memories of itchy, infected welts on the skin tend to fade like the scars, being replaced by only wistful reminiscences of paradise lost.

*        *        *

Ideally situated next to our motel was the rather discerningly named sports bar, 'Helen Back' - do you get it? I must admit it took me longer than it should have.

We entered via the rear of the building which actually features a large terrace overlooking the sea. The interior was just what one would imagine a sports bar to be like. A large central bar with accompanying bar stools catered for the solo clientele in need of some human interaction, surrounded by tables and chairs for diners and a stage for live entertainment. There was also a large games room and a separate hall with a large screen, I presume for the big games.

If your mission is to meet the locals or others just travelling through then one needs only to plonk ones derriere on a bar stool and you immediately become fair game for conversation. Given the friendliness of your average American, these bars can be an invaluable source of local information and a great way to pass an evening.

We pulled up some bar stools and were immediately greeted by a friendly, cheerful twenty-something-year-old girl with a lovely smile and a pair of those legendary long tanned legs. Her costume was designed by someone who obviously doesn't credit the everyday sports bar customer with a lot of imagination which, after having looked at middle-aged men all day, was fine by me. The experience was only slightly marred by the presence of her co-worker, a mountain of a man with long hair, pock-marked face and a passion for tattoos that would shock even the most masochistic premier league football star. He audibly snarled like a hyena in our direction every time we said anything to our bargirl other than "four more beers please" and after a short while we relented and found a table a safe distance away.

One may ask how a bar full of people that are so evidently not sporty gets its name? Well, it's all to do with the numerous televisions hanging from the walls and ceilings, continually broadcasting live national and international sporting action. The three large screens in front of us featured a padded rugby game (known there as American football), a men's netball game (I think they called it basket ball) and a rounder's match (known there as baseball or something like that), with the combined entertainment value of your average freshly painted wall.

Fortunately, half way through the evening the resident DJ fired up his equipment and played some great music. When the time came to eat, the young waitresses unknowingly entertained us, thinking nothing of exhibiting a few spontaneous, synchronised dance moves when an appropriate tune came on. As one not always appreciative of the fine dining experience, I found this evening of lively conversation, pizza, nachos and cold larger wholly agreeable.

# *Eighteen*

I awoke after a fitful sleep. However much I may complain about the cold winters of central France, I don't think I could ever voluntarily live in a climate so warm as to necessitate sleeping in an air-conditioned environment for the majority of the year. The aircon' unit in this motel room was particularly hard to live with. For a start, it seemed determined to single-handedly take us into the next ice age, with no amount of control panel manipulation having any effect whatsoever. Secondly, the fan produced the kind of decibels easily comparable to the firing of a Boeing's engines during acceleration for take-off. Lastly, every time the unit kicked in, it made a noise reminiscent of a bird hitting a car wind-screen at great speed. All in all an atmosphere not entirely conducive to sleeping but, after a hearty breakfast by the pool with a stunning sea view, the night's escapades were quickly forgotten.

After much debate, using the motel wifi we managed to book our next hotel at Panama City beach so, without further ado, we packed the car and headed out on the scenic Route 98 coastal road.

We reached Panama City just after mid-day and checked into our hotel before heading straight to the beach to catch some rays.

The coastline consists of a beautiful, white sandy beach that seemingly goes on forever and the area is highly developed with tall blocks of condominiums and plenty of retail outlets and restaurants. We decided to head a little further out of town to find a quieter spot. Stepping out of the air-conditioned car and on to the white hot sand it was obvious that if our beach visit was to have any kind of longevity, we had to find some shade. The only option available was a conveniently placed pier and so we set down our towels along with two hundred other people in the narrow strip of shade under the board walk. After a stroll up and down and even a swim in the luke warm water, I decided that the occupants of this beach were not the Floridian's advertised on TV. Nowhere to be seen were the glamorous youth with bodies like bikini models or pectorals you could grate cheese on. The majority of the beach, excluding the four pale, moderately· overweight English dudes, could be categorized into two groups. The immensely fat Afro-Americans with their tiny children (it was easy to imagine who ate all the pies at their houses) and the also obese, tattooed red-neck descendents of very pale European settlers, often sporting sculptured facial hair. Both groups made an art of hollering threats at their children, who seemed to have built up a very effective immunity to any parental advice on offer. I sat and observed, bathing when I felt my blood was on the verge of boiling and feeling secretly thankful that the 'baby' stage in our lives had come and gone without incident. I can still remember taking our children to the beach. I can still recall playing in the waves and building sand castles, but fortunately the memories of the logistical nightmare of carting around all the stuff needed for an enjoyable day on the beach has faded. OK, we make a lot of fuss about our children being potty-trained, learning to walk and talk etc, but I truly believe that the real breakthrough in a parent's life comes when children develop the strength to carry their own stuff around. Have you ever been skiing with small children? I have and it is the closest I have come to a cardiac arrest to date. It is the combination of carrying several pairs of skis and poles, walking miles up hill in crippling ski boots and wearing clothing that raises the body temperature to near fainting level, whilst all the time trying to convince your kids that they aren't suffering from frostbite and they will eventually have fun. And all this takes place in an environment prone to sporadic changes in weather, producing what can only be described as life threatening situations. Talk about irresponsible parenting!

We stayed until our skin couldn't take anymore and then retreated to a nearby bar where I sampled a copious shrimp and crawfish po'boy, washed down with a couple of bottles of Dos Equis. Neil and I returned to the beach for another swim and enjoyed an amazing Florida sunset whilst my brother and Alex paid a small fee for the pleasure of a walk on the pier. They came back jubilant, having witnessed fishermen reeling in and gutting a number of large king mackerel just off the shore.

*     *     *

After freshening up back at our hotel, we left our car and ventured out into the night on foot in search of some action. As usual we seemed to be the only people walking out that night which led me to the question, is your average American just lazy or are we incredibly naïve and could at any moment be subjected to a mugging or drive by shooting every time we leave the safety of our vehicle?

We headed to a neon-lit bar known as The Wicked Wheel bar and grill. This all-American bikers' bar boasts not only real Harley Davidson bar stools but also a number of beautifully polished machines dotted around the place. We pulled up our, by now customary, bar stools and struck up a conversation with a couple of local ladies and the bar staff. By way of an amuse bouche we were presented with peanuts boiled in spicy sea water, a combination that I found intriguing. The soggy peanuts were served piping hot in their shells and were actually quite messy to eat due to the ejaculation of hot salty liquid when the nuts were released. Finding the taste not to their liking, my friends offered me their nuts and I swallowed mouthful after mouthful of the salty treat until I felt quite sick. For no apparent reason an image of Marc Almond has just popped into my head.

After a short tour of the various superbikes on display, we meandered over to the dining tables for some supper. I ordered a burger with succotash, which up until this point in my life had no other meaning than to be an exclamation of hardship by Sylvester, the cat of Looney Tunes fame. However it seems that succotash is not only edible but also good for you, made primarily from sweet corn, shelled beans, tomatoes and peppers and containing lots of amino acids, whatever they may be. I can also verify after a windy night that it also smells remarkably similar in gas form.

With our bellies fit to burst, some exercise was in order and so we decided on an evening stroll to the sea front, where we stumbled upon Pineapple Willies bar. We ordered a beer and had a look around the place. The bar was half full of what I imagined to be college kids and all eyes were intermittently transfixed on a large screen showing a football game. During the brief moments when something actually happens during a game of American football, there were raucous cries and I could tell by the expletives flying around that the home team wasn't doing very well. The atmosphere was a far cry from the friendly bar we had just left. In fact on this particular night, with a little artistic license, I could have compared it to the bar in the Jodie Foster film, *The Accused*. Although I'm sure we were in no danger of ending up like poor Jodie's character, we decided to call it a night and headed back to the hotel.

# Nineteen

This day was to be the longest drive of the trip, over seven hundred kilometers down to Sarasota. However, things didn't start well when we awoke to find a crack in our car windscreen about twelve inches long. At first we thought somebody had tried to vandalize the car but, on closer inspection, it appeared to start from a tiny chip that my brother had noticed when we first hired the car. At this point I had a déjà-vous moment. I had been in a car which had suffered the same fate and, as far as my addled brain could recall, it was due to the vast difference in temperature between the air-conditioned interior and the blazingly sunny exterior. After a brief study of the insurance contact we were none the wiser as to if we were covered or not, so we decided to not let it mar the day.

First stop of the day was on the outskirts of Tallahassee for fuel, burgers, wifi and vain attempts to book a room in Sarasota. We then witnessed the not everyday occurrence of crossing a time line, taking us to GMT minus five. Being the self-proclaimed creators of modern time and inhabiting a tiny island, this is not something that the English ever have to consider but it must make life interesting to live next to a time line. If you fancy spending another hour in bed, surely you just get a job over the line and start life an hour later? With a three hour time difference from east to west, does this mean that long-distance lorry drivers suffer constantly from a form of mini jetlag? Roadlag, possibly?

There's not a great deal to see whilst on the motorways of Florida but one thing that is ubiquitous to the region is the oversized, roadside billboard featuring crisp photos of smug men with Jewish sounding names. Smiling for the camera with impeccably placed hair, they advertise all types of aggressive legal action and I'm sure they would be capable of suing their very mothers for the right fee. It's no surprise that people are reluctant to intervene in any kind of contentious situation through fear of getting caught up in a law suit. Thanks to these lawyers, we have to think twice before taking other people's children to sports events in our car, making a cake for the local fete (for fear of poising somebody with an allergic reaction) or lending a tool to a neighbor and risk him hurting himself and blaming the tool. I knew a baker once in England that had built up a thriving business until one day an employee had an accident that could have been avoided with a little more care. The employee sued the baker, the baker went bust and four people lost their livelihoods, including the person that sued. Who is the winner in this situation? It can only be the blood-sucking lawyers. In the U.S. it is even worse. I remember befriending a waiter in Minnesota who had planned to rent a car with three friends for a trip to Florida. He had to pull out for financial reasons and his three so-called friends took him to court for his part of the car rental. Is that really how friends behave? Do people really choose what amounted, in this case, to a negligible amount of money over friendship? I guess in some cases they do.

We soldiered on down the Interstate 10, watching the crack in our windscreen miraculously creep across the entire width and eventually reached Sarasota late afternoon to begin the search for accommodation. Eventually we found a motel a little out of town that complied with both Neil's exacting standards of quality and my low budgetary requirements. We dumped our stuff and headed into town in search of sustenance.

The first appealing bar we came to was Smokin' Joes. As the interior was fairly busy we pulled up some bar stools on the terrace looking into the bar. I was amazed to see people sitting inside smoking humungous cigars and cigarettes, something I thought was illegal almost everywhere but apparently not here. After a day cooped up in the car together, we downed our beers in comparative silence before moving on to find something more solid to ingest.

Primarily in search of ambiance, all the restaurants in the area were conspicuously empty and so the criteria changed to the most affordable place which happened to be a Mexican restaurant. We were speedily seated and provided with plates of delicious nachos and beans whilst waiting for our order to arrive. The waiter placed a large pot on the table containing chicken, beef, prawns and Cactus, the latter being another first for me but not something I necessarily need to try again.

We tried in vain to find some night life but it seems that outside the big cities, there isn't a great deal of demand, so we retired to our motel to console ourselves with some humorous YouTube clips.

# Twenty

I awoke again after a restless night's sleep due to an ancient air-conditioning unit and convened with the others at the breakfast table to discuss apartments in Miami.

Neil loves Miami and, having visited several times before, recommended that we stay as close as possible to the famed Miami Beach. Unfortunately for me this was also one of the most expensive parts of town with prices easily double that of our usual budget. After a much heated debate and haggling, we finally found a lovely apartment one block back from Ocean Drive but still too expensive for Alex and myself. A deal was cut when my brother and Neil generously agreed to pay an unequal share of the fee and we waited nervously as Neil called to make the booking. The news was all good and we instantly relaxed in the knowledge that we didn't have to waste another afternoon scrambling around to find a bed.

I backed the car up to the motel and started to load our bags into the boot. Standing in the doorway, a movement caught my eye and I turned to see a vagrant approaching our luggage with his arm out ready to strike. He hadn't seen me in the doorway and when I jumped out and questioned his motives he put his hands up in defence, as if he expected a good kicking. "Hey, what's up?" I questioned, to which he speedily improvised "Hey man, I just wanted to tell you your trunk was open" The guy, although clearly proclaiming his innocence, was very apologetic anyway, even telling me to 'have a nice day' as he shuffled away. I must admit that being a cynic normally excuses me from charitable acts but something about his humble politeness touched me and I found myself running after him and pressing some dollars into his grubby hand. Even though he was probably going straight to the liquor store or his local dealer, it still gave me a little glow and the tiniest inkling of what it might be like to be Father Christmas.

We ploughed down Route 75, stopping for fuel in a local gas station where nobody appeared to speak English and feeling like we had inadvertently changed countries. As we descended deeper into Florida, it was evident that in many areas Spanish was the preferred language of choice. We turned onto Route 41 through the vast, flatness of the Everglades, passing through Alligator Alley and following the signs to Miami.

I had previously visited Miami all those years ago as part of my tour of the States but, in fact, remember very little about it. I had hitched a lift with a couple of girls from New Orleans who had rented a car and I can vaguely recall being dropped off in what must have been downtown. I stayed in a hostel and after a couple of days on the beach, left for the Florida Keys. My most vivid memory of the city twenty-five years ago was a diner selling ninety-nine-cent fried breakfasts, a thought that I still find appealing.

As we approached the imposing high-rise blocks which mark downtown, I recognized nothing from my previous trip.

Legend has it that the name Miami originates from the Mayaimi tribe, a group of Native Americans that settled around lake Mayaimi, (meaning 'big water') now known as Lake Okeechobee. Up until the late 1800's, the settlement, that is now a city, remained small but some harsh winters in the 1890's highlighted the area's benefits. Much of the Florida harvests were wiped out during this period by frost but the extreme south was unaffected. Miami was popularized as 'frost proof' and, with the arrival of the railroad in 1896, the area witnessed a period of rapid growth and expansion.

One of the biggest influences on the region has been its proximity to Cuba. During Cuba's tumultuous history, hundreds of thousands of Spanish speaking immigrants have flocked to the region, giving the city its Hispanic feel. During the 1960's, a massive influx of Cuban refugees pushed out many of the non-Hispanic whites in a period known as 'White Flight'. Large populations of Afro-Caribbean's have also influenced the area creating a Latin-Caribbean feel. In the 1980's, Miami became one of the main gateways for trafficking cocaine from Colombia, Bolivia and Peru, a practice glamorized in TV shows such as 'Miami Vice'. Since then, the city has developed a global image synonymous with expensive cars, sun-kissed beaches and beautiful people.

We passed the island known as Star Island, although as far as I know the only star that resides there is Gloria Estefan. She was born in Havana and, along with her family, fled Cuba during the revolution. Following global success in the music industry, hers is another 'rags to riches' story, the epitome of the American dream. It truly looks like a wonderful place to live with its palatial mansions and immaculate gardens, all basking in glorious sunshine.

As we pulled into Miami Beach, it was evident that the area was going to live up to its reputation. My first reflection whilst driving around in search of our apartment was that, up until now, I had never seen more than one Lamborghini at a time. I witnessed five in the first five minutes, including three parked in a row outside a rather swish looking hotel.

We found our apartment block, entered into the sumptuous reception and were led to our accommodation, past a tropical bar next to an ample swimming pool. Things were really looking up for the last days of our holiday!

We dumped our stuff and explored the apartment. Two en-suite bathrooms, a balcony with a view, sumptuous sofa and enormous flat screen TV, all in all not too shabby. First stop was to be the beach and, after all the hype I had seen over the years, expectations were running high. We donned our beachwear, grabbed our towels and power walked the short distance to the coast to be confronted with the enormous expanse of fine white sand that forms Miami Beach. After so many hours in the car, I had no interest in lying in the sun but when I professed an interest in walking the length of the beach, I was greeted with rather cynical jeers from my fellow compatriots. They, obviously oblivious to my real nature, accused me of wanting to ogle at young ladies in string-wear, an idea that I found not singularly abhorrent. When I insisted that my premier concern was a vain attempt to walk off a few of the beers and burgers we had consumed during the trip, I was greeted again with unfair skeptical glances. Anyway, in direct defiance of the Miami 'keep our beaches sexy' association, the shirts came off and an unreasonable volume of sun cream was applied.

We meandered up the coastline with the waves lapping at our feet, sandwiched between the warm waters of the Caribbean and a bevy of thong-clad beauties and rippling beef basking in the sun, well on their way to a perfect tan. Taken at face value, this really did seem like a lot of peoples' idea of paradise with not an obese or old person in sight, except of course us. We couldn't escape the tattoos though. When I was young, a tattoo was a fairly extreme symbol associated with either someone in the armed forces or else people living on the fringes of society, such as prostitutes or aggressive young men laden with sadistic tendencies etc. An open advertisement that the person in question either surrendered to a sudden urge to make a permanent declaration of love for a mother, girlfriend, animal etc, usually under the influence of alcohol. Or is dogged with the kind of self-loathing that leads to voluntary self-mutilation. There was always somebody at school or down the pub with a botched homemade tattoo, the most popular being love and hate etched onto the knuckles. Although these people had their place in society, it was not normally a place that the majority of the population wanted to share with them.

I guess it is because of that that I find it hard to look upon this latest fashion objectively (by Jove, we really do turn into our parents). Along the beach, there were a number of young women and men with designs that start at the feet and run the whole length of the body.

Personally, I'm afraid the effect from a slight distance leaves the same impression as a facial piercing, which could easily be mistaken for a puss ridden spot, or a jeweled tooth replacement which I'm afraid just looks like a rotten tooth. These vast tattoos viewed from a few meters just looked like badly scarred skin, a poor substitute for the perfect, natural skin beneath. I'm sure that there are many that disagree with me but I cannot help feeling relieved that I come from a generation where being different seemed less important than fitting in and physical adornments were less permanent. The irony as always is that if everyone does it, tattoo-free skin will become the next fashion and what will this generation do then? I remember a similar craze in the nineties when the young trendy's got their noses pierced in order to look a bit different from their mates. It happened to coincide with the time I was travelling in India and, guess what, virtually every English backpacker I met had a nose piercing, making me stand out without even trying.

As we continued up the beach, I fantasized about what it must be like to be young, healthy and rich on this planet. I wondered if these Lamborghini-driving play boys are any happier than me and my friends. I had a spell in my youth of cruising around in a Ford XR3 with a couple of mates attempting to impress the ladies. Admittedly it's not a Lambo' (but let me tell you it was quite sought after at the time), but then Kent isn't quite

Miami Beach either. Anyway that thankfully small period of my life was certainly not the happiest. For peace of mind I choose to believe that we all have our limited capacities for happiness and misery and no amount of external stimulus (except maybe a shit loads of drugs) can change this. I just hope I'm right and these bastards are not on a happy plain ten stories above my own.

We paused a moment to slap a litre or so more of the super factor sun cream on, the kind that taints the skin white, like an emulsion paint, just to totally eradicate any remaining semblance of cool that we thought we might still possess. Walking back towards civilization we hit Ocean Drive, a name that I cannot even think of without starting to hum the famed ditty by the now obscure band 'The Lighthouse Family'.

By now it was late afternoon and people were milling around trying to decide which bar offered the best happy hour cocktails or which of the waitresses' outfits revealed the most flesh. But no such dilemmas for us as we headed back to the apartment complex for a swim and a shower.

On Neil's recommendation we gravitated back to Ocean Drive for the evening in search of food and entertainment. The street is famed for its Art Deco style architecture including a house that even I recognized. It was the beautiful beach front villa, Casa Casuarina, owned by the late Italian fashion designer Gianni Versace. I can still recall the news coverage and the global outcry that followed his death. He was gunned down on the very steps outside this house on the first of July, 1997, aged just fifty years old. The killer took his own life eight days later taking with him any possible motive for the assassination. The building now operates as a luxury hotel but I can imagine a little over our budget.

We ran the not wholly unpleasant gauntlet of attractive street hecklers, many appearing to be of Eastern European or Russian descent.

I couldn't help but make a comparison between these people and the breed of heckler I came across during a stint as a tour rep' in Magaluf many years ago. Their job was reliant on their ability to fill up the many bars in the so called 'Shagaluf' and, in my experience, were all sunshine and light until it become evident that you were not taking them up on their kind offer of two-for-one shots off of a dwarfs armpit. This usually prompted a reaction to the tune of a deftly mouthed 'wanker' at a speed and volume which makes the insult hard to substantiate.  It always seems a little bizarre to me that people with such an obviously dislike of rejection should choose such a desperate vocation.

However this was not the case on this particular night tonight due to the fact that your average Ocean Drive heckler is in a different class.  Adorned in elegant eveningwear, rejection was taken with a friendly smile and a request that we enjoy our evening.

We settled into a bar by the name of 'The Clevelander' selected by Neil, which coincidently featured waitresses sporting not much more than underwear. I think having daughters myself made me feel a little uncomfortable with ordering my drinks from someone with so little clothing on, but after I realized that they were totally relaxed about it, it ceased to be a problem. In fact, in the still roasting evening temperature, the uniforms seemed very practical.

We all went for beer except Neil, who ordered one of the gigantic cocktails on offer. They really are in a glass the size of a bucket and are probably meant for sharing but our friend was on another mission.

Ordering a second round, a couple of wealthy middle-aged women sat down on the table next to us. By now Neil's cocktails were definitely making headway in his bloodstream and his speech had a soupçon of a slur to it. He launched into an epic tale of how Alex and I were musicians about to hit the big time with our band. One of the ladies responded by saying that her daughter was dating one of the Motley Crew or some band like that, and if we wanted she would pass on a demo. Talk about bad timing; I would have killed somebody (OK maybe maimed them a little) for a break like that thirty years ago! When one of the ladies said that she was here as a treat to help get over the death of her husband I felt terrible that our friend was taking them for a proverbial ride. The only redeeming feature of that little escapade was that when the check arrived it was easily large enough to hide my embarrassment. After apologising profusely when Neil began to fill the air with expletives, we left the confused ladies to their cocktails and moved on.

I refused to pay the astounding cover charge and minimum spend to gain entry to the next bar and so Alex and I decided to abandon the evening's entertainment, leaving Neil in the capable hands of my brother.

We strolled down the street in search of coffee, entertained by boy racers accelerating their super cars to the maximum that one can when sandwiched between two sets of traffic lights a block apart. I'm sure one nearly got into second gear at one point before slamming the brakes on at the last second, smoke billowing from the wheels. I don't think speed was the real issue but more importantly the idea was to make as much noise as possible to advertise the fact that they or at least someone in the family could afford a car like that.

As we passed some of the more glamorous Art Deco hotels the dulcet tones of the ladies of the night floated out from the shadows, "Hi boys, anything I can do for you?" or "Do you need anything special tonight?" I was tempted to ask her to pay my mortgage off but I restrained myself.

All the cafes were shut, so we meandered back to the apartment to raid the complementary drinks shelf.

I awoke with a start in the middle of the night as all the lights came on at once. Neil and my brother had returned but I was too tired to be bothered with the finer details of their evening so I dosed off into an imaginary world of untold luxury and privilege.

# Twenty One

No sign of Neil at breakfast so my brother filled me in on the previous night's adventure. After we had left, they moved on to a bar called Mango's featuring live entertainment in the form of dance and cabaret. Fueled by even more alcohol, Neil became out of control and started filming various parts of the dancing girls at close proximity. The evening came abruptly to an end when he accidently stumbled against one of the bar girls, forcing her to call security and escort him out. It's not very often that I make the right decision when it comes to alcohol but as Neil arrived late for breakfast looking like death warmed up, I couldn't help but feel a little smug.

The breakfast was by far the best we had experienced, with bottomless cappuccinos and a vast choice of delicious hot and cold food. I decided to eat as much as I liked and worry about the consequences later. Dining by the poolside in the warm Miami sunshine is definitely an experience I'd like to get used to.

Today was a big day. Although I had visited the Everglades before, I had never experienced the celebrated airboat ride, venturing out into the alligator infested wilderness. After studying the various options on line, we made our choice and headed out of Miami on Route 41. We chose a company called 'Buffalo Tiger's Airboat Rides' located in Alligator Alley, for three reasons. Primarily, it is situated a little more than an hour's drive from Miami; secondly, it wasn't necessary to reserve a time as it works on a first come first serve basis; and finally, it is owned and run by Native Americans which we hoped might add an element of authenticity to the trip.

After running the gauntlet of exiting Miami during rush hour with a crack in the windscreen now large enough to impair vision, we arrived a little flustered. The reception was not much more than a wooden shack packed with alligator memorabilia but the friendly staff sold us tickets and we took our place in a small queue by the airboat moorings. During the short wait for the boat to return, I read up a little on the area.

Somewhat unimaginatively named the River of Grass because of the abundance of saw grass in the area, the Everglades are basically a network of interconnected ponds forming a gigantic flowing marshland. In an area renowned for wildlife, it is reportedly unique as the only place that alligators and crocodiles can live side by side, due to the mixture of fresh and salt water. The Everglades at one time covered more that eleven thousand square miles of Southern Florida but is now, like most natural habitats throughout the world, in danger of destruction. Effective drainage schemes have laid much of the land to agriculture but what is left of the ecosystem has been made into a National Park, hopefully insuring its continued existence for future generations.

As we stood in line we caught our first sighting of a wild alligator, patrolling menacingly close to the timber moorings, daring us to approach the bank for that perfect close up photo. Obviously we had all seen 'Crocodile Dundee' and knew how devious the blighters can be.

My heart accelerated a little in anticipation as a distant hum amplified to a roar and I caught my first glimpse of the returning airboat, speeding across the marshland before cutting the motor and gliding into the jetty. Our guide gave us a rundown of what we were likely to see and a list of safety instructions which really boiled down to IF YOU WANT TO SEE YOUR KIDS AGAIN KEEP EVERYTHING IN THE BOAT. With this clearly understood, we were handed our ear protection and took our places on the boat with around twenty other European tourists. Looking around I couldn't help but remark on the fact that the boat looked like it had been fashioned out of wafer thin aluminum, powered only by an old car engine driving a makeshift propeller bolted onto the back. I'm sure it was a state of the art machine but given our location, personally I wasn't overwhelmed with that warm feeling of security. Still it is their business and I didn't notice any chalk lines or notches indicating passengers lost and so I relaxed.

As the powerful engine fired up and we accelerated out into the wilderness I was impressed that, rather like a hovercraft, the boat worked equally well on both marshy grassland and water. Our guide took the boat up to a good speed, every now and then broad-siding to the left or right in an attempt to terrify us, eventually cutting the engine and gliding to a halt on some reed beds. For a moment all was quiet, eyes fixed on the murky water around us. Within minutes we had several alligators of varying sizes circling the boat. The largest female, obviously used to these little visits, hauled herself out of the water and sat on the reed bed virtually touching the boat. She was a healthy two meters long and judging by her teeth, quite capable of lunching on anyone of us. To my amazement, a Dutch family virtually stuck their cameras in the beast's mouth without so much as a thought of the potential consequences – obviously Australian films never got as far as the land of windmills. Our guide gave her a little bread (the alligator, not the tourist) and she seemed quite relaxed as he stroked her snout, making large clucking noises for no apparent reason - maybe it's an Indian thing. He pointed to various parts of her anatomy explaining how it all works and ran through the lifecycle. Around the beginning of April, the male will start his courtship process by bellowing, creating deep vibrations in the water and possibly blowing bubbles. The females make huge nests between seven and ten feet in diameter and proceed to lay up to ninety eggs which are covered and guarded for the next nine or ten weeks. Rather bizarrely, the sex of the 'gator is determined by the temperature of the nest, low temperatures produce more females and higher temperatures more males. When the young are ready to hatch, they cry from the egg to alert their mother that it's time. The young then stay with mummy for a year under her protection until she has to start the process again. In the early years, mortality rates are as high as eighty percent and the little creatures are ranked pretty low down the food chain. This situation is soon reversed as they grow to adulthood, with a natural lifespan of up to fifty years.

The guide sparked up the engine and we zoomed off again, stopping a few minutes later in what appeared to be a random spot. This time the waters were still with no apparent life in the immediate vicinity. It soon became apparent why. From a few meters away, a huge male surfaced and laboriously hauled his bulk out of the water to settle immediately beside what now seemed like a flimsy little boat. He was a truly magnificent beast and I noticed with satisfaction that not even the Dutch were brave enough to attempt a close-up. He sat there, waiting for one of us to stick our arm or leg out but, when it became apparent that we were too well trained, he dragged himself slowly back into the water and disappeared in the murky depths. What I found slightly unnerving is that even though he must have been very close, he was completely invisible, not even an air bubble to mark his position.

I couldn't help but wonder how many settlers had inadvertently fallen prey to these stealthy killing machines over the centuries. Apparently a few weeks before a twenty-eight year old jogger went missing, only to be found in an alligator's belly a few days later. Our guide informed us that once caught in the jaws of an alligator, death comes in the form of blood loss, trauma and drowning. The 'gator then rolls with the victim to break off parts of the body, before swallowing them whole. I can think of better ways to go....

Next stop was a reconstructed Miccosukee Indian village. The boat glided up to the moorings and we all mooched down the gangway in the blistering Florida heat. With all eyes on a central construction of branches and grass, we were distracted by a slight rippling sound in the water behind us. We turned to see a large 'gator furtively climbing out of the water rather in the manner that a cat stalks its prey. The whole group immediately gravitated away from the danger, and I managed to position myself behind a Dutch child, optimistic that the beast would naturally prefer lamb to mutton. Our guide reacted by calmly persuading the animal to retreat with a threatening looking stick and, crisis over, the tour continued. As we followed the decked pathway through a wooded area, we were greeted with an array of wildlife, from beautifully coloured birds to over-sized insects. Something that resembled a grasshopper distinguished itself to us Europeans by being all of four inches long, nearer the size of a bird than an insect.

Gathering in the safety of the boat we were told the story of the man responsible for the creation of the airboat company.

William Buffalo Tiger was chief and political leader of the Miccosukee Indians, a tribe based in Southern Florida. He spent a lifetime fighting for the recognition of his tribe and regained rights to self-govern in their native lands, the Everglades. He started the airboat company to generate wealth for his people and to educate tourists as to the importance of preserving this unique environment.

As we headed back to the relative safety of solid ground, I must admit that I was somewhat relieved that I don't have to contend with such a hostile environment on a daily basis. After a quick look at the souvenirs it was time to jump back into the air-conditioned haven that was our car for the drive back to Miami, narrowly avoiding a tenacious vulture unwilling to leave his lunch of road kill.

We fought our way back across the city and breathed a sigh of relief when we eventually got back to our apartment block. By now mid afternoon, I felt a sense of urgency to get back to the beach to catch a few rays to hold me in good stead for the approaching long French winter. My companions joined me and we swam and lounged about on the glorious sand until sunset. Neil demonstrated his photographic dexterity when he managed to capture my brother and me in the sea with the silhouette of a pelican flying over our heads.

The light gradually ebbed away and it was time to retreat to the apartment to freshen up for what was to be our last night out of the trip. In the time it took to shower, a violent storm materialized and, as we prepared to leave, it was evident that venturing out onto the streets would probably result in a drowning or two. So we made ourselves comfortable in the complex bar, ordering food and beer and watching rain of a magnitude that I have rarely witnessed. The pool was quickly over flowing and the courtyard resembled a large pond and then, as quickly as it had materialized, the storm dissipated to reveal a perfect starry night.

We paced up the waterlogged streets onto Ocean Drive and headed to Mango's, a bar that both my brother and Neil highly recommended. By this stage in the trip I was all but penniless but not for the first time the richer amongst us stepped up to the mark and generously acquiesced to pay the cover charge and buy some beers. I am, contrary to public opinion, somewhat unaccustomed to accepting such charity due probably to an ill-conceived notion of male pride, but on this occasion I was intrigued to see what all the fuss was about.

Mango's is one of those places where the bar staff double up as entertainers or perhaps it's the other way around judging by the quality of the entertainment. One minute you are being served by a beautiful bar girl in an elegant dress or a shirtless hunk with muscles on his muscles. The next minute they could be up on stage performing a hot salsa, break dancing or robotics, maybe doing a little Whitney Houston number or a perfectly choreographed rendition of a Michael Jackson song.

Although there is a possibility that my brain might have been addled by extortionately priced lager, the whole evening was incredibly entertaining from a variety of perspectives. The ambiance was greatly ameliorated by the clientele, many of whom were Hispanic. They appear to be blessed with an incredibly sensual, effortless understanding of rhythm which I'm sure must be learned in the womb as mummy gently sways her bump to Gloria Estefan. They also seem to have an almost psychic ability to start swaying in unison at apparently random moments during a song. I have vague recollections of a cycling tour of Andalusia with the lady that became my wife many years ago. We happened upon many festivals featuring large numbers of people often wearing traditional attire and standing around in the city squares listening to music. All at once, the crowd would start stamping their feet and clapping their hands like Mick Jagger, spinning around in time to the music as if their very lives depended on it, only to stop minutes later and stand around casually until the next impulse overcame them. I found it all totally bemusing but, at the same time, thoroughly endearing, and I thank goodness that cultural differences still exist to spice up our lives in our increasingly culturally homogenous world.

Anyway the Mango's clientele brought their *joie de vivre* and their best dance moves and greatly added to my enjoyment of the soirée.

I stood spellbound for the majority of the evening until the alcohol stealthily crept up on me. The result was that my feet began to move in what felt like a smooth rhythmic flow but what was probably a series of chemically induced, uncontrolled spasms. What is it with Northern European men and dancing? To my mind we can be clearly divided into two groups – group A: those who take the trouble to actually learn to dance, practicing individual moves in front of the mirror for hours on end. This method can work but the results are often stilted as the person in question attempts to connect a series of rehearsed moves to a variety of different rhythms and music. The resulting dance might be an over-energetic performance, often attracting too much attention i.e. everybody forming a circle around our hypothetical dancing queen and clapping in unison until one has exhausted ones repertoire. Then there is group B: In this group, the majority of us feel like we need some sort of chemical stimulant in order to strut our stuff. Why does the very thought of taking to the floor strike fear into our hearts? Is it through some misguided notion that we may ridicule ourselves? Let's face it, if you turn down the music and watch your average night crowd jerking about, doesn't everybody look a bit silly? I can only presume that it is learnt from our elders, in much the same way as our famed English reserve is assimilated. In any case, on this particular evening, I would have willingly sold my small collection of Russian stamps for an injection of that Hispanic rhythm into my stiff Anglo-Saxon veins.

I found well into the evening that the beers were no longer quenching my thirst and it struck me that after sixteen nights of overindulgence I had finally had enough. It must be time to go home. The others felt the same and so we meandered back to the apartment for our last sleep on American soil.

After another luxurious breakfast, we had one thing left to do before heading out to the airport for our evening flight home. We packed up our things and jumped into the car heading south out of the suburbs, sandwiched between the enormous expanse of the Everglades wilderness and the vastness of the Ocean. We were taking the U.S Highway 1, otherwise known as the overseas highway, which would in fact make a great future road trip. Running from Fort Kent in Maine, 2370 miles down to Key West, it is the longest North-South road in the United States.

The road became increasingly surrounded by bodies of water, finally passing over the Blackwater Sound, the Gulf of Mexico to our right and the Atlantic Ocean to our left. We had reached our destination. All that remained was to find a nice spot preferably with coffee and reflect on our journey.

The very presence of the Florida Keys is somewhat fascinating. They were part of a massive coral reef which formed many thousands of years ago when sea levels were a lot higher than they are currently, a period of time when southern Florida was actually under the ocean. As sea levels dropped the coral fossilized, forming an archipelago extending more than a hundred miles out into the ocean. The area experiences only two seasons ranging from hot and humid to cooler and drier and there has never been a recorded frost. For many years Key West was the largest European settlement in Florida, the inhabitants profiting from the many shipwrecks in the area. Unluckily for them the income dried up, primarily due to technical advances in navigating during the late nineteenth century, resulting in fewer accidents.

My first inspiration to visit Key Largo came not from the film but from the Beach Boys song 'Kokomo'. When I listened to this song as a student, it conjured up images of a beach paradise, but the reality is always different. If there is one thing that I have learnt from travelling, it is that paradise exists only in the mind. External stimulation can only take us so far down the road and then it's up to us to bridge the gap with a positive mentality. For me at this moment, paradise didn't come in the form of our location, although the diner we stopped at did have a certain charm. No, for me the moment came during the consumption of my last American breakfast, consisting of eggs over-easy, smoked sausage, potato cakes, bacon and toast, served with coffee and a smile. This I was going to miss.

We walked down to Cannon Beach, aptly named as it features both cannons and a beach – did you know that contrary to my previous utopian mental image of the Florida Keys, they have very little in the way of natural beaches. However, this one was pleasant, with the added attraction of a replica of a shipwrecked Spanish Galleon sunk out in the bay to entertain divers and snorkelers.

We lounged around on the beach trying desperately to say something profound about our experiences together over the previous three weeks, but in actual fact just looking forward to going home to our families. So we headed back to the airport for the last of our challenges before the flight, to convince the insurance company that the crack in the wind screen was not our fault.

It turned out that the guy at the airport accepted the car with no fuss and we proceeded to the terminal in high spirits. As we sipped on a last beer at the airport gate we experienced one of those strange, almost surreal moments in life. For a start, my brothers team, Arsenal, were beating Tottenham in a cup tie rather bizarrely on the bar TV and then, for no apparent reason, my brothers phone started playing 'Dirty Water' by the group 'The Inmates', a song about a man's love for his home town, London. Could this be the spirit of that great city telling us that it was time to return? I would like to think so.

# Twenty Two

We left Florida as we had found it, bathed in sunshine and busying itself with daily routine. The flight back seemed shorter this time, as being at night made it much easier to sleep. As we approached Heathrow, a thought entered my mind that, as far as I can remember, I have never landed in London and not been greeted with grey sky or rain. Taxiing to the terminal, I watched the raindrops bouncing off the airplane wing and the ground crew sporting waterproofs and I was missing the U.S. already. Couldn't we just turn around and go do it all again?

A short taxi ride back to my brother's house and we were greeted with a kiss from my sister-in-law and a grunt from her teenage son and before long we were drinking tea and thinking about kick-starting our family lives.

My sister-in-law asked us if in hindsight if we would have done anything differently. In fact, the only stress was caused by not pre-booking all the accommodation. By allowing ourselves a margin of freedom to be spontaneous we were actually more constrained – not always finding accommodation in the right location for the right price. We lost time trawling through websites and driving around towns looking for a place to stay, although I'm sure many would view this as part of the fun. It would also have been nice to spend more time in the small towns in order to sample more of the real America but I guess we'll just have to go back again one day!

We all agreed that the trip had been a roaring success and that we needed to do something like this again before old age quells our desire to travel.

As I left to catch my flight home my brother called out "How about a train trip around the world?"……..

18867166R00111

Printed in Poland
by Amazon Fulfillment
Poland Sp. z o.o., Wrocław